To Ed A. Gray

With appreciation for your
life and work.

Batul Barrett Baxter

When
Life Tumbles In

When Life Tumbles In

Conquering Life's Problems

Batsell Barrett Baxter

BAKER BOOK HOUSE
Grand Rapids, Michigan

Contents

Preface

During forty years of active ministry, fifteen of which have included a national radio and television program, "Herald of Truth," I have known many people *in times of crisis.* Some have stood like the Rock of Gibraltar; others have been shattered. These messages are designed to help those who are passing through crises and to prepare the rest of us for such situations ahead.

I owe a debt of gratitude to many people for the materials that help to make these messages meaningful, but am especially indebted to the writers and researchers who assist me on "Herald of Truth."

Vast resources of help to those in difficult situations of any kind are available from the Christian faith, from God's Word. I hope this book will help many people discover these resources *for times of crisis.*

1

The Temptation
of Suicide

Some time ago I read of a young girl in England who leaped to her death from the high window of a famous cathedral. This was another tragic case of one who found life not worth living. A few minutes before a young man in New York leaped to his death, he said, "I wish someone could convince me that life is worth living." The police who were there tried to convince him. Others spoke to him as he was perched on the promontory of the building, but it was all in vain. The crowd below watched as he plummeted to his death on the sidewalks.

Statistics indicate that twenty-thousand times each year here in the United States someone takes his own life. That's fifty-five people every day, more than one every half hour. Suicide has become the tenth ranking cause of death in our nation, and one wonders why. What are the causes?

Sociologists and psychiatrists tell us that one of them is serious physical illness or the fear of it. Others are financial reverses, frustration, loneliness, and purposelessness, or lack of aim in life. But far more basic than any other one cause is the inability to give and to receive love. Man's failure to love and to be loved does devastating things to the tender human heart. This brings

9

to mind I Corinthians 13, which the apostle Paul closed with the words, ". . . now abideth faith, hope, love, these three; and the greatest of these is love."

Factors That Break Us Down

Let's take a closer look at some of the difficulties and sufferings that cause men to break down and take their own lives. Visualize with me some imaginary, yet typical, real-life situations.

You had a long drive ahead of you so you started early, before the roads became clogged with weekend traffic. You and your wife had been looking forward to this vacation for a long time. As you waited for the first rays of dawn to light up the sky, you recalled the old saying that it is darkest just before the dawn.

Suddenly, out of nowhere, blinding headlights careened around a curve and headed directly toward you. You swerved to avoid a collision, but as you did, you felt yourself going off the road.

In the last split second of consciousness, your only thought was of your wife. When you regained consciousness, it was morning and a lot of people surrounded you—policemen, ambulance attendants, curious spectators. You were bleeding profusely and you knew there were broken bones. You didn't have to ask how serious your condition was; you could see it reflected on the face of the policeman.

But what of your wife? Where was she? And how seriously had she been hurt? You finally caught sight of her. She appeared to be all right. You heard the ambulance doctor ask if she could walk to the ambulance and you were relieved to see that she could. If anything happened to Emily, you asked yourself, who would take care of the children? How thankful you were that the kids were not in the car. You hadn't liked the idea of leaving them with their grandmother, but how fortunate that you had.

All the way to the hospital, Emily didn't say much. She seemed to be in a state of shock, but the doctor kept reassuring you both that she didn't have any broken bones and that there were no bruises or signs of bleeding. Relieved that your wife had been spared, you began to pray for your own recovery.

You were totally unprepared for what happened. You didn't actually learn the details until weeks later when you were strong enough to leave the hospital. One minute, your wife had been sitting calmly on the bench, waiting for an examination. The next, she was dead. There had been no outward visible marks that would even remotely indicate she had been mortally injured. The medical examiner said she had died of shock. *Your* wounds had been ugly and obvious . . . but you eventually recovered. *Her* wounds were hidden within . . . and she succumbed!

The vice president's job in your firm is open. As sales manager and a forty-year employee of the company, you consider yourself the best-qualified person for the position. And, after all the time you've put in, promoting you to vice president is the least they can do.

The telephone rings. It's the call you've been waiting for. The president of the firm wants to see you in his office. As you head for the executive offices, you review in your mind the short acceptance speech you have prepared for this occasion.

He greets you warmly, then tells you in confidence that a merger is about to be announced, that the president of the other company will become the new senior vice president, and that he is bringing his sales manager with him. All you remember after that is his offer of an early retirement. As he paints a picture of leisure and well-deserved rest, you are certain of only two things—you have been eased out and your pride has been wounded.

You're getting on in years and, living with your married daughter and her family, you've begun to feel useless and unwanted. But today is your proudest day; you've just won first prize for the best needlework at the county fair. You can hardly wait to get home and tell the family. But when you do, you find that nothing has changed; the kids are too busy to listen to an old woman, and even your daughter is too involved with preparing dinner to share your good news. You were floating on air just a moment ago, but now you are completely deflated. Your ego has been deeply wounded.

When you saw the advertisement in the newspaper, it sounded like the kind of safe investment the two of you were looking for to insure your future security. But, when it became obvious to you that the man you were dealing with was a fraud and that you were going to lose your life savings, you took the swindler to court. Now, you sit in total disbelief as you watch the defendant's lawyer cleverly get around the law on technicalities.

Despite your lawyer's efforts, you know your case is crumbling and that the defendant will get off, scot-free. Your savings are gone; you've been shown to be a trusting fool; you feel crushed by a big, impersonal, uncaring society.

Has anyone reading these words never been hurt by resentment, jealousy, pride, injustice, or misunderstanding? Perhaps you were able to cover up your injuries with a smile and a shrug of the shoulders, but what of the inner wound? "The spirit of a man can endure his sickness," Solomon wrote in his Book of Proverbs, "but a broken spirit who can bear?" (18:14 NASB).

The seventeenth-century dramatist John Lyly wrote: "The wound that bleedeth inwardly is most dangerous." These words are just as true now as then, despite the tremendous advances in medicine. We know how insidious cancer can be—eating away at healthy tissue while the body appears to be healthy. The dangers of glaucoma are just now being publicized. Special equipment is needed to detect the harmful build-up of pressure within the eyeball. But there are other kinds of inner wounds to be concerned about—wounds of the spirit which we all suffer at one time or another. The first-century Latin poet Virgil put it this way: "The secret wound lives on within the breast."

Surmounting Our Difficulties

The philosopher Immanuel Kant said that the dove might consider air resistance a problem, something to be overcome, but without it the dove couldn't fly. Even our modern jets must take off against the wind, getting maximum resistance from the air. Yes, it is true that resistance is difficult to overcome; yet that same resistance is what makes flying possible, both for the dove and for our planes. I'm also convinced that resistance is what makes triumphant living possible.

The opening lines of Milton's "Paradise Lost" point to the source of all human problems and, at the same time, to the divine solution:

Of man's first disobedience, and the fruit
Of that forbidden tree, whose mortal taste
Brought death into the world, and all our woe,
With loss of Eden, till one greater Man
Restore us, and regain the blissful seat ...

Milton himself was a pawn in the raging political controversies of his time. His employer relieved him, an experience many of you have shared. Then came a much greater blow—the loss of his sight. But he did not lose hope, nor did it diminish his zeal for learning.

Left in solitude, Milton began work on his monumental "Paradise Lost." It was the work of his declining years. "It was produced," writes his biographer, "when every turbulent feeling of youth had subsided; when experience had had her perfect work, and when his soul could listen in quiet to the voice of the charmer, Wisdom." The work was completed in 1665 when Milton was sixty years old, long tortured by illness, suffering the terrible deprivation of blindness, bereft of his companion, and financially straitened. While most of his writings and those of succeeding ages have been forgotten, Milton's pure lines endure.

Centuries before Milton, Paul—that indomitable soldier of the cross—wrote of his own suffering. Tradition tells us he was frail, and sacred history mentions his "thorn in the flesh" (II Cor. 12:7), but there was in this great man of God no frailty of spirit. Thus we find him saying, "We are pressed on every side, yet not straitened; perplexed, yet not unto despair; pursued, yet not forsaken; smitten down, yet not destroyed" (II Cor. 4:8, 9).

At another time, Paul compared the struggle of life to athletic competition, a passage translated by Phillips in unusually sharp and compelling language: "Every competitor in athletic events goes into serious training. Athletes will take tremendous pains—for a fading crown of leaves. But our contest is for an eternal crown that will never fade. I run the race then with determination. I am no shadowboxer; I really fight! I am my body's sternest master, for fear that when I have preached to others I should myself be disqualified" (I Cor. 9:25, 27).

The apostle Paul suffered many things for Christ's sake. He said: "Of the Jews five times received I forty stripes save one. Thrice was I beaten with rods, once was I stoned, thrice I suffered shipwreck, a night and a day have I been in the deep; in journeyings often, in perils of rivers, in perils of robbers, in perils from my countrymen, in perils from the Gentiles, in perils in the city, in perils in the wilderness, in perils in the sea, in perils among false brethren; in labor and travail, in watchings often, in hunger and thirst, in fastings often, in cold and nakedness" (II Cor. 11:24-27).

What a list of sufferings! Yet, he also said that "I take pleasure in weaknesses, in injuries, in necessities, in persecutions, in distresses, for Christ's sake: for when I am weak, then am I strong" (II Cor. 12:10).

Paul's language is not that of a quitter or a chronic complainer. The Christian refuses to be a loser, even in the face of diminishing physical powers, or waning social and family contacts, or crippling disease, or outrageous treatment, or even by the approach of death itself. Paul's language is that of a winner, one who confidently affirms that "I have fought the good fight, I have finished the course, I have kept the faith: henceforth there is laid up for me the crown of righteousness, which the Lord, the righteous judge, shall give to me at that day; and not to me only, but also to all them that have loved his appearing" (II Tim. 4:7, 8).

Paul's words bring to mind a godly man and woman who both recently retired, he from a lucrative business and she from teaching school. The man can be described as moderately well-fixed financially; his health is good, his interests are many, and he contributes his skills to the church, free of charge. But he has been severely tried. His beloved wife, who seemed to be in the best of health, left the house one day to attend a luncheon.

He never saw her alive again. A massive stroke was fatal. In the few lucid moments that remained before she lost consciousness, she faced death unwaveringly. Later her husband was heard to say, "I am glad she was able to die with dignity, and more so that she died in the Lord."

I have confidence that in all the lonely hours in store for this man, now bereft of his beloved companion of more than forty years, he will not succumb to futile rantings about the supposed injustices of God. Rather, like Job, he will be able to say, ". . . the Lord gave, and the Lord hath taken away; blessed be the name of the Lord" (1:21 AV). Then there are those magnificent lines from the pen of the prophet Ezekiel: "I spake unto the people in the morning; and at even my wife died; and I did in the morning as I was commanded" (24:18).

No Promise of Freedom from Suffering

Our Lord never promised that those who follow Him would be free from suffering and pain. He never promised perpetual good health or financial prosperity. Rather, He said, ". . . If any man would come after me, let him deny himself, and take up his cross, and follow me. For whosoever would save his life shall lose it: and whosoever shall lose his life for my sake shall find it" (Matt. 16:24, 25).

Just as difficulties and sufferings sometimes break men down— although they need not—so do affluence and luxury. Too many people put too much emphasis upon material things; and, when something happens to their material things, they break down. They need to learn from Jesus that ". . . a man's life consisteth not in the abundance of the things which he possesseth" (Luke 12:15). They should say with Solomon,

> . . . Give me neither poverty nor riches;
> Feed me with the food that is needful for me:
> Lest I be full, and deny thee, and say, Who is Jehovah?
> Or lest I be poor, and steal,
> And use profanely the name of my God.
>
> [Prov. 30:8, 9]

The apostle Paul said the same thing in different words: "But godliness with contentment is great gain: for we brought nothing into the world, for neither can we carry anything out; but having food and covering we shall be therewith content. But they that are minded to be rich fall into a temptation and a snare and many foolish and hurtful lusts, such as drown men in destruction and perdition. For the love of money is a root of all kinds of evil: which some reaching after have been led astray from the faith, and have pierced themselves through with many sorrows" (I Tim. 6:6-10).

We Americans who grew up in the twentieth century have been brainwashed by the highly-touted success formula: individual effort is rewarded by outstanding achievement and happiness. Such is not the case for millions who appear destined to miss the objectives that once colored their dreams.

Perhaps the dream has faded in your life. At one time, you may have felt the realization of your dreams was very near— only to have all hope fail as a result of greed or trickery or some meandering mischief that chanced to come your way. Then, with opportunities gone and the march of years about to engulf you, bright hopes were replaced by bitterness and self-pity—the evil twin sisters of spiritual destruction.

The negative, despondent, destructive attitude toward life is not so much imposed by our circumstances as by our reactions to those circumstances. Some who have very little thank God for what they have, and some who have much are nevertheless despondent and disturbed. Some are crushed by life; others are challenged by it.

Four Rules for Happiness

I want to suggest four rules for living that will help you attain peace of mind and happiness, that fulfillment of human destiny that all of us seek.

First, *depend upon God*. God is in His heaven. God still rules in the affairs of men. The God who marks the sparrow's fall, the God who knows the number of the hairs on our heads, is concerned for our good; we need His guidance. It was Jeremiah who said, "O Jehovah, I know that the way of man is not

in himself; it is not in man that walketh to direct his steps"
(Jer. 10:23).

David said, "Yea though I walk through the valley of the
shadow of death, I will fear no evil; for thou art with me; Thy
rod and thy staff, they comfort me" (Ps. 23:4). The last words
that our Lord spoke while on earth, according to our record,
are these: ". . . lo, I am with you always, even unto the end of
the world" (Matt. 28:20).

The Christian can also be comforted by these words: "In
nothing be anxious; but in everything by prayer and supplication
. . . let your requests be made known unto God. And the peace
of God, which passeth all understanding, shall guard your hearts
and your thoughts in Christ Jesus" (Phil. 4:6, 7).

The greatest deterrent to suicide is a strong Christian faith.
Such faith enables a man to bounce over the rough spots of
life, to meet the tensions and stresses. I think that we need to
go again to the apostle Paul to observe the faith that gave him
a resilience to life's problems. He wrote, "We are pressed on
every side, yet not straitened; perplexed, yet not unto despair;
pursued, yet not forsaken; smitten down, yet not destroyed"
(II Cor. 4:8, 9). Several verses later Paul adds: "Wherefore we
faint not; but though our outward man is decaying, yet our inward man is renewed day by day. For our light affliction, which
is for the moment, worketh for us more and more exceedingly
an eternal weight of glory" (4:16, 17).

The second rule for fulfillment and happiness is, *accept your
lot*. Accept pain and suffering and disappointment as well as the
good things of life. I know it's difficult to accept poverty when
those about us are wealthy. I know it's difficult to accept illness
or suffering when those about us are in robust health. And, yet,
it's possible. It's possible if we can accept God's values. Sometimes things are not as bad as they appear, and sometimes they
are not as good as they appear. By looking through God's eyes,
as it were, we can accept our lot.

Hebrews 11:24-26 tells us, "By faith Moses, when he was
grown up, refused to be called the son of Pharaoh's daughter;
choosing rather to share ill treatment with the people of God,
than to enjoy the pleasures of sin for a season; accounting the

reproach of Christ greater riches than the treasures of Egypt."
On the surface, Moses made a very bad choice. Here was Egypt
with power and prestige and wealth, and there was Israel in
slavery. And, yet, he made a very good choice: in Egypt there
was idolatry and sensuality that would have ruined Moses; with
Israel he found a challenge to real greatness.

We need not only to accept God's set of values but also to
remember God's promises. Only by remembering God's promises
could the apostle Paul say, ". . . I have learned, in whatsoever
state I am, therein to be content. I know how to be abased, and
I know also how to abound: in everything and in all things have
I learned the secret both to be filled and to be hungry, both to
abound and to be in want. I can do all things in him that
strengtheneth me" (Phil. 4:11-13). And so we can learn to
accept our lot in life.

The third of our rules is very simple: *live in the present.*
Wrote Sir William Osler in his book, *A Way of Life:* "If the
load of tomorrow be added to that of yesterday and carried today, it will make the strongest falter. Live in day-tight compart-
ments. Don't let yesterday and tomorrow intrude on your life.
Live one day at a time. You'll avoid the waste of energy, the
mental distress, the nervous worries that dog the steps of the
man who's anxious about the future." That is exactly what our
Lord said in the sermon on the mount: "Be not therefore
anxious for the morrow: for the morrow will be anxious for
itself. Sufficient unto the day is the evil thereof" (Matt. 6:34).

A friend who is the editor of a large metropolitan newspaper
recently told me that in the course of one year he's expected
to write something like one thousand editorials. "If I saw them
all in a row," he said, "I would say it was impossible. But when
I think of just two or three or possibly four for tomorrow's
issue, why, then I can handle the problem all right."

If the housewife could see the hundreds of miles of floor
that she must sweep during the rest of her life or the mountain
of dishes that she must wash, she probably would be completely
unable to begin. But if she can wash just the dishes after one
meal and then after another meal, she can handle her problem.

Even our children learn to live in the future. The preschool child, instead of enjoying his freedom, wants to start school, then to be in first grade. And then he wants to be in the second grade. Pretty soon he wants to be in junior high school or high school; and even college doesn't satisfy long, because a young person wants a job. Then he wants to marry; wants a house; wants a family. We look toward retirement. Before very long, life is over and at the end of it we look back and see how we've robbed ourselves by living in the future. We need to live each day as it comes.

Yesterday's gone, and it's gone forever. Tomorrow may never come, but you have today. Use it. Don't waste it. Savor it. Enjoy it. There'll never be another day just like this one; and, when it's gone, it'll be gone forever. Our prayer should be:

> Lord, for tomorrow and its needs,
> I do not pray;
> Keep me, my God, from stain of sin,
> Just for today."

And now we come to our fourth rule: *aim for worthwhile achievement*. In other words, live for a purpose. Viktor Frankl, the noted psychiatrist, told about his experience in a concentration camp some years ago in a now-famous book. He and several thousand other men were herded into a large enclosure. They were fed once a day; food was brought in one large container and left in the middle of the field. The men soon began to behave like animals; whatever veneer of civilization they'd had soon wore off. After several weeks, some went insane and some died. But the ones who survived were the ones who had purpose, a goal that enabled them to keep their sanity.

The apostle Paul achieved some great things in his life, for he had a goal which was the very center of his being. "Brethren, I count not myself yet to have laid hold: but one thing I do, forgetting the things which are behind, and stretching forward to the things which are before, I press on toward the goal unto the prize of the high calling of God in Christ Jesus" (Phil. 3:13, 14).

Yes, Paul had a purpose, but neither he nor any other person has ever had such singleness of purpose as our Lord. Even before He was born, it was said, ". . . he shall save his people from their sins" (Matt. 1:21). And we are made aware of His love and purpose by John 3:16: "For God so loved the world, that he gave his only begotten Son, that whosoever believeth on him should not perish, but have eternal life."

Is life worth living? Admittedly, there are times when one has to wonder. Life has its problems—mistreatment by one's fellowmen, loss of possessions, serious illness, death, and many more—but life also has its strengths. As we've just seen, when our lives are undergirded by a strong faith in God and the Lord Jesus Christ, we have the resources to survive anything.

When life's joys are put on the balance with its sorrows, I confidently believe that the former will outweigh the latter. After God created the universe and everything in it, the Scriptures tell us that "God saw everything that he had made, and behold, it was very good" (Gen. 1:31). It is still good—very good. Life is worth living!

2

The Problem
of Loneliness

Never have people been so close to one another—yet so far apart—as we are today.

Our world is shrinking into a community of nations who now recognize that their problems and needs are intertwined. A political upheaval in the Far East affects nations in the West. Social upheaval in the Southern Hemisphere affects the stability of society in the Northern Hemisphere. Supersonic travel brings widely separated nations within hours of one another. Communications satellites have made possible visual contact between not only various sections of the world but also the earth and the moon.

Individuals are experiencing something similar. We live in apartment complexes which resemble small, self-contained cities, work in crowded office buildings, and spend many of our recreation hours in huge stadiums.

But powerful *divisive* forces also seem to be at work in our world. Wars and conflicting ideologies separate the international community. Race, class, and age divisions create wide gaps within our society. Bargaining between labor and management regularly results in economic disruption. Homes are dramatically divided by separation and divorce. Crowded together—yet living in empty loneliness!

When Jesus was born, there were only about 250 million people in the world. Today, more than three and one-half billion share this planet and, unless the birthrate changes dramatically, there will be more than six billion of us by the year 2000!

The rate of population growth in the United States is lower than it was a few years ago, but our population will increase by forty-five to sixty million people between 1975 and 1985. Most of this growth is taking place in our cities where an average of three thousand acres of green land is being bulldozed daily. Almost one-third of the population of the United States lives in some fifteen metropolitan areas. The growth in these areas means that, every year, a new city of two million must be built to accommodate the exploding population of the United States.

Yet tremendous crowds of people living together have not resulted in "community" among these people. In fact, it seems to have done just the opposite to us. Our restless mobility is indicated by the fact that nearly twenty percent of Americans move every year. Our craving for amusement—reflected in the expansion of the spectator sports, as well as in the less healthy trends toward the sensuous in movies and literature—is a surface indication that we are not a contented people.

There are deeper indications of our loneliness. Our national divorce rate indicates serious loneliness in the home where relationships with others should be the most meaningful. The prevalence of suicide suggests a terrible loneliness within the human spirit.

Has anyone never known the agony of loneliness and the ache of emptiness? This dangerous emotion has been called the problem that plagues more people these days than any other. An eminent Swiss psychiatrist calls it "the most devastating malady of the age." And a distinguished physician recently stated, "There is no human condition so acute—or so universal."

Loneliness, of course, is not a unique symptom of the 1970s. In 1934 the well-known journalist and humorist, Don Marquis, wrote: "All religion, all life, all art, all expression come down to this: to the effort of the human soul to break through its barrier of loneliness—of intolerable loneliness—and make some contact with another seeking soul, or with what all souls seek, which is (by any name) God."

Loneliness Is Universal

In a sometimes hostile world, in times of enforced separation (as in the case of a boy whose military service has taken him to the other side of the world, away from home and family and friends), or neglect (as in old age), or the death of a loved one, loneliness can be a gnawing, agonizing experience. A disturbing sameness in letters left by suicides points to loneliness as one of the chief causes of self-destruction. The elderly especially feel the burden of loneliness. Lord Byron helps us feel the full impact of this aloneness in one of the stanzas of "Childe Harold":

> What is the worst of foes that wait on age?
> What stamps the wrinkle deeper on the brow?
> To view each loved one blotted from life's page,
> And be alone on earth, as I am now.

Thomas Wolfe described the magnitude of the problem of loneliness, even in his day: "The whole conviction of my life now rests upon the belief that loneliness, far from being a rare and curious phenomenon, peculiar to myself and to a few other solitary men, is the central and inevitable fact of human existence."

As I see it, there are two kinds of loneliness. The first we may call the *isolation of space*. This is the boy, far away from home and loved ones, fulfilling his military obligations in Germany, or Iceland, or Korea, or Viet Nam. How he longs to be home again! Letters mean so much. Memory keeps the human ties alive and strong. This loneliness of space is also felt by the businessman away from his family four nights of the week as he works his assigned territory. This is also the loneliness of parents whose children are grown and now live in some other part of the country. How they look forward to the brief trips home, to a few days with children and grandchildren. There is something deeply satisfying in being close to those we love and who love us. There is reassurance in the physical touch—the embrace, the kiss, or even just the touch of the hand, or the glance of the eye. When apart we like to "keep in touch" by telephone, or by letter, or by sending snapshots or gifts. As painful as the separation of distance is, it has one saving feature: even though separated from us by space there are those who love us and with whom we will be reunited. Our hearts are strengthened when we remember their earnest longings which rise up to heaven for us daily.

The other kind of loneliness, and far heavier to bear, is the *isolation of spirit*. This is the loneliness of the city and of the crowd. "There are times when hands touch ours," wrote Frederick W. Robertson, "but only send an icy chill of unsympathizing indifference to the heart: when eyes gaze into ours, but with a glazed look which cannot read into the bottom of our souls— when words pass from our lips, but only come back as an echo reverberated without replying through a dreary solitude—when the multitude throng and press us, and we cannot say, as Christ said, 'Somebody touched me;' for the only contact has been not between soul and soul, but only between form and form."

"No Man Cares"

The lonely person may decide that his unhappiness is peculiar to persons in his age group, or in his social class, or in his race. However, these external factors, by themselves, do not cause loneliness. Loneliness strikes without regard for age, place, or condition.

It can even affect the very young whose parents have too little time for them. Teenagers are not immune, especially today. Many feel misunderstood and alienated from their elders, and since the new generation has yet to find answers to many of man's needs, there seems to be no one to turn to. There is the loneliness within marriage, where many couples feel estranged from their partners even while living together in the most intimate of relationships. Most poignant of all is the loneliness of the aged who often feel useless and unwanted. No one is immune. There are the lonely poor and the lonely rich, the lonely blacks and the lonely whites.

Have you thought of the cross section of personalities in the Bible who must have experienced deep loneliness? Think of Moses who had to flee Egypt after killing a man; David, who found it necessary to hide in a cave because King Saul was pursuing him; Elijah, who thought he was the only man left in Israel who opposed the introduction of Baal worship; the prodigal son, who was reduced from wealth to serving in a swine pen; Peter, who went out into the night to weep bitterly after denying Christ; Paul, who had to send his close associates to visit and help young churches while he remained virtually alone in a Roman prison. All of these must have known moments of deep loneliness.

The clue to what loneliness really is can be found in that line from Psalm 142, "No man cares for my soul." Loneliness is the feeling of being cut off from other people, deserted, or banished from their company. It is not the mere fact of being physically alone; it is the result of a breakdown in the emotional giving and receiving between people. We humans need the support of friendly relationships with others as badly as we need food and drink, and when we are denied satisfying relationships with other people, the result is loneliness.

We may be in a crowd, or we may live in the same house with other people, but if we withdraw into our individual shells and build walls to separate us from others—even though the walls may be invisible—we become lonely.

Residents of one community—Davenport, Iowa—have done something about this universal problem. Some years ago, they inaugurated a phone service known as Dial-a-Listener. At the receiving end is a rotating staff of volunteers who keep the number open around the clock. At the calling end are the lonely people of Davenport who hunger for the sound of a sympathetic human voice. Unlike the numerous Dial-a-Prayer switchboards and suicide-prevention centers, the purpose of Dial-a-Listener is neither to deliver canned messages of hope nor to cope with life-and-death crises, but simply to offer lonely callers a human connection.

The volunteers—who range from school teachers and nurses to authors and engineers—are carefully screened for the qualities that will survive the impersonality of the telephone; namely, a warm, sympathetic voice and, above all, the willingness to listen.

While a service like this is commendable, it is only a stopgap. The permanent solution to loneliness lies in a personal, one-to-one relationship with people. But, sometimes, circumstances may contribute to the breakdown of these relationships with others.

There are those who, through circumstances, must live alone and spend a good deal of time by themselves, but who are seldom lonely. These people usually have a strong sense of self-esteem; they think of themselves as good company. These are men and women who live full and useful lives, who make worthwhile emotional investments in other people and activities.

One such person is a gallant lady I read about recently. She lives alone and is crippled by arthritis, yet she keeps up a huge correspondence with those who need cheering up. The contagion of her joyous spirit is reflected in this statement of hers: "I have spent many a day alone but never a lonely day."

We may at times be forced into a position of being alone by the death of a companion, or by our children leaving home for the responsibilities of their own adulthood, or by moving into a strange community. If we allow ourselves to grieve because of our losses, or to become afraid in our new circumstances, or to engage in self-pity because we are physically alone, real loneliness may set in.

There are times also when one must stand alone—swim against the current. The apostle Paul began the ethical section of his letter to the church at Rome with an appeal for non-conformity—a challenge to stand for the right even when it means standing alone. "I appeal to you therefore, brethren, by the mercies of God, to present your bodies as a living sacrifice, holy and acceptable to God, which is your spiritual worship. Do not be conformed to this world but be transformed by the renewal of your mind, that you may prove what is the will of God, what is good and acceptable and perfect" (12:1, 2 RSV).

Standing alone against the sweeping current of one's time can be lonely. Responsibilities may dictate that one be alone while making crucial decisions.

The presidency of the United States has often been called

"the loneliest job in the world." The feeling that "the buck stops here," in the words of one recent president, suggests a feeling of "aloneness" in important decisions that must be made, and which often involve millions of people. Abraham Lincoln once observed, "I have been driven many times to my knees by the overwhelming conviction that I had nowhere else to go. My own wisdom, and that of all about me, seemed insufficient for the day."

A Fundamental Anxiety

This brings us to the most pathetic loneliness of all—trying to live separated from God. Life has no real meaning apart from Him. The greatest single evidence of loneliness today is the number of people who express a complete lack of purpose in life, an emptiness, a basic meaninglessness about human existence.

There is a fundamental anxiety at the very foundation of life, which is inseparably related to our feelings of loneliness. Man was created in the image of God. He is the offspring of God, the child of God. In the beginning there was companionship with God—a closeness between Creator and creature, between Father and child. Then came man's desire for freedom. He went his way rather than God's way. An estrangement between God and man resulted, an estrangement caused by man's sin. Ever since, there has been a longing in the heart of God for man's return. This is the message of the prophet Hosea; it is the message of Christ in His story about the prodigal son. There has also been a loneliness in the heart of man—a loneliness so deep that man has seldom understood it or seen clearly the way to remove it. Man has gone his way of so-called freedom, missing the deepest joy of all—a rich relationship with God, his Maker—and suffering the anxiety of loneliness. This is what Augustine meant when he said, "Our souls are never at rest, until they find rest in Thee."

From this deep kind of anxiety and loneliness man has sought escape. His escapism has taken many forms: love of sex; the use of drugs; bizarre dress; defiance of religious, community, and world standards. None of these, or the many other escapes, has brought satisfaction. Man, by himself, cannot find the calmness of spirit, the peace of mind, which he craves. What he needs is not *escape,* but *return.*

As Adam and Eve, after their rebellion against God, tried to hide themselves, so modern man is still trying to run away from God, to escape. He needs to return to God and to a new and different kind of life. In the words of Fulton Sheen, this new life brings "spiritual, moral and mental security found through being enfolded in the meaning and goal of life . . . It is law, order, rhythm, pattern, purpose. It is a philosophy of life; it is the revelation not only of where I came from, but also of where I am going. Inscape [as he calls it] is the discovery of order and meaning; it means being wrapped in the cloak of the mystery of God; the making oneself intelligible and giving life a meaning; it is finding a refuge in the God of love. For every escapism there must be inscapism; for every flight from reality, there must be a return to it; for every lost personality, there must be its recovery."

Listen to these words from Admiral Richard E. Byrd, which appeared in his book, *Alone,* words written during his five lonely months in the Antarctic while gathering scientiflc information.

> I paused to listen to the silence. My breath, crystalized as it passed my cheeks, drifted on a breeze gentler than a whisper. The wind vane pointed toward the South Pole. Presently the wind cups ceased the gentle turning as the cold killed the breeze. My frozen breath hung like a cloud overhead. The day was dying, the night was being born— but with great peace. Here were the imponderable processes and forces of the cosmos, harmonious and soundless. Harmony, that was it! That was what came out of the silence—a gentle rhythm, the strain of a perfect chord, the music of the spheres, perhaps. It was enough to catch that rhythm, momentarily to be myself a part of it. In that instant I could feel no doubt of man's oneness with the universe. The conviction came that, that rhythm was too orderly, tco harmonious, too perfect to be a product of blind chance—that, therefore, there must be purpose in the whole and that man was part of that whole and not an accidental offshoot. It was a feeling that transcended reason; that went to the heart of man's despair and found it groundless. The universe was a cosmos, not a chaos; man was as rightfully a part of that cosmos as were the day and night.

When man returns to God, both in the material universe and in the moral realm, he discovers that his deepest anxiety and his deepest loneliness have gone. He experiences an inner joy and buoyancy of spirit described by the apostle Paul as "the peace of God, which passeth all understanding." And this peace "shall guard your hearts and your thoughts in Christ Jesus" (Phil. 4:7).

The Loneliness of Christ

Anyone who is very familiar with Christ's life senses the deep loneliness which He often felt. Rejected by the prominent and powerful leaders of His day, misunderstood by the masses which constantly surged around Him, and only partially understood by His closest disciples, He often felt alone. He felt this solitude in the desert, in Pilate's judgment hall, in the garden, and especially on the cross. A few days before His crucifixion, as the multitudes left Him, He asked His disciples, "Would ye also go away?" (John 6:67). On the night of His betrayal, He said to His sleepy apostles, "Sleep on now, and take your rest: behold the hour is at hand . . ." (Matt. 26:45). They had slept while He agonized over the fate of the world. On the cross, while dying, he uttered the cry, "My God, my God, why hast thou forsaken me?" (Matt. 27:46). He had to walk the path to the cross alone.

Undoubtedly, Jesus' capacity for suffering was greater than that of any of us. His great heart of love, which reached out to all mankind, especially the poor and downtrodden, must have felt the full force of the anguish of loneliness. In His loneliness, occasioned by the great temptations (Matt. 4), He was one against the entire world. The prophet Isaiah wrote concerning the Messiah, "I have trodden the winepress alone" (63:3). Christ trod the winepress alone and triumphed over principalities and powers by Himself (Col. 2:15). There was no man with Him; for when He entered the lists with the powers of darkness, all His disciples forsook Him and fled. There was none to help, none that could, none that would, but there were many to oppose and to hinder. Yet, Jesus provided us with the key to triumph over loneliness when we face our problems. Jesus said to His disciples, "The hour cometh, yea, is come, that ye shall be scattered, every man to his own, and shall leave me alone:

and yet I am not alone, because the Father is with me" (John 16:32). Knowing that He was doing God's will, He could solidly depend on God's nearness to Him. This is our strength in times of loneliness, too. In His final recorded words to the apostles, as recorded in the Gospel of Matthew, Jesus said to all of those who would follow Him down through the ages, "Lo, I am with you always, even unto the end of the world" (Matt. 28:20). When loneliness threatens to overwhelm us, the realization that our Lord is near strengthens us to live meaningful lives.

Abide with Me

I have found the following paragraphs from the book, *Light from Many Lamps,* a source of strength.

> Henry Francis Lyte walked into his study...an old man... near the end of the journey. He was tired and ill. The doctor told him that he had only a few months to live. He thumbed the well-worn Bible on his desk and it fell open at one of his favorite passages: "Abide with us; for it is towards evening and the day is now far spent." In the quiet of his curtained study, he read and reread those familiar comforting words.
>
> And all at once he was no longer old and tired! All at once he was no longer sad and burdened, no longer discouraged! Words sang through his mind; and he put them down on paper; and in less than an hour he had written one of the most beautiful and inspiring hymns of all time: "Abide With Me."
>
> When the famous nurse, Edith Cavell, went before a German firing squad, she whispered the words of "Abide With Me." When the HMS Stella was sinking with 105 victims during the Second World War, a woman—one of the noble unidentified of the world—stood on the bridge and sang "Abide With Me" until the others were singing with her, and they went down bravely.

We are reminded of Paul's great statement to the Romans, "If God be for us [or with us], who is against us?" (8:31).

As did our Lord, we also will likely face our sternest tests when alone. That's when temptations are at their strongest. Sometimes base and vicious inclinations conflict with those that are pure and holy. Even more difficult are those conflicts between two virtues, forcing us to choose the better of the two.

When the temptation and the lower nature struggle for mastery, we can usually muster the strength to overcome them by the combined force of spiritual values; but our greatest tests often come when we have to struggle between two loyalties, both of which may be praiseworthy. When obedience to our heavenly Father, for example, requires disobedience to an earthly father, we face the most difficult kind of struggle. Jesus forewarned us of this when he said, ". . . a man's foes shall be they of his own household. He that loveth father or mother more than me is not worthy of me . . . And he that doth not take his cross and follow after me, is not worthy of me. He that findeth his life shall lose it; and he that loseth his life for my sake shall find it" (Matt. 10:36-39). Sometimes even a much-loved friend must be met with "Get thee behind me, Satan," as Jesus once addressed Peter. It is often when human advice is unavailable that the soul learns what it means to be alone.

Ultimately, alone, each of us must make the major decision of his life—the decision whether to follow Christ and live for the Spirit, or to follow the world and live for the flesh. Herein lies our greatest battle. Will our lives be lives of loneliness, or will they be lives of fulfillment, eternally satisfied by the peace of God?

Nearly three thousand years ago David wrote the 121st Psalm, in which he revealed that he had grasped the secret of finding peace with God.

> I will lift up mine eyes unto the mountains:
> From whence shall my help come?
> My help cometh from Jehovah,
> Who made heaven and earth.
> He will not suffer thy foot to be moved:
> He that keepeth thee will not slumber.
> Behold, he that keepeth Israel
> Will neither slumber nor sleep.
> Jehovah is thy keeper:
> Jehovah is thy shade upon thy right hand.
> The sun shall not smite thee by day,
> Nor the moon by night.

Jehovah will keep thee from all evil;
He will keep thy soul.
Jehovah will keep thy going out and thy coming in
From this time forth and for evermore.

3

The Deadening Effect
of Frustration

Frustration has the dubious honor of being near the top of the list of the giant, negative, destructive emotions that plague mankind. Frustrations are of many kinds. Some are relatively unimportant: one's friend is late for an appointment; one loses his house key; one's car breaks down just when he's in a great hurry. Far more significant frustrations are these: a teen-age girl is so plain in appearance that no one asks her for a date; a teen-age boy who has set his heart on making a certain team is cut; a much-wanted job goes to someone else; bad grades result in being dropped from college; the economic level of one's friends and neighbors proves unattainable. Perhaps deeper yet is the frustration that comes when a person realizes that he's got a serious physical illness, or perhaps some permanent physical handicap, or maybe it's a mental handicap. The truculent son, the wayward daughter, the brutish husband, the nagging wife, the querulous grandparents—all of these bring frustrations.

At the side of the bed of a departed loved one, there's a stunned silence, and then the heart-rending cry of disappointment and bewilderment. Many a man or woman in such a circumstance has said, "Why did this have to happen to me?"

A hard-working, self-sacrificing wife has a husband who squanders his pay each week on liquor, leaving his family to make out the best they can in their privation. This goes on week after week, month after month, year after year. There's no realistic hope for change. Out of her slough of despondency, the wife cries, "Why? Why? Why?"

Or maybe it's a hard-working man who's cut down in the prime of life by some major illness. No longer is he able to hold his job. Now he cannot provide even food, clothing, and shelter for his children, much less the education that he'd dreamed of. And, in his despair, he says, "What must I do?"

Frustrations are of many kinds and of varying intensities. Seemingly there is no place in life, there is no time, no circumstance in life, that is immune to frustration. And whether they be the minor, day-to-day frustrations or giant, life-crushing frustrations, they come when one's plans are thwarted or goals are made unattainable. They come when the toy a baby has been playing with is taken away, when a youngster who dreams of playing ball in the big leagues is cut from the high school team, when a woman who is deeply in love with someone realizes that he is not in love with her.

One young woman put it this way: "I'm tired of living. I want to die!" This was when she discovered the consequences of her rather careless kind of life. She'd intended a gay, carefree, happy life, and now she saw that the future held something very different. Perhaps facetiously, someone else has said, "Stop the world! I want to get off."

It's intensely interesting to study the way people react to their frustrations. But it's even more than that. It's of tremendous value to see the different ways that different people respond to their disappointments.

Meeting Disappointments

The circumstances around us are important in determining our behavior. But far more important than these circumstances, these external things, are the principles within us which determine how we meet disappointment and frustration.

Some become very angry, venting their anger upon themselves, upon their associates, sometimes even upon God. But anger never accomplishes anything; it only makes matters worse.

A little more than eighty years ago, the great Scottish preacher Henry Drummond delivered a sermon that was destined to be the most widely printed of any sermon in the English language. From that sermon comes this paragraph: "No form of vice, not worldliness, not greed of gold, not drunkenness itself, does more to un-Christianize society than evil temper. For embittering life, for breaking up communities, for destroying the most sacred relationships, for devastating homes, for withering up men and women, for taking the bloom off childhood; in short, for sheer gratuitous misery-producing power, this influence stands alone."

Others respond by giving up, by quitting. They blame their failures on their unfortunate circumstances. Eventually they despair. Some of them enter hospitals for the mentally ill. Some of them take their lives. But many more simply live on in self-pity, making everyone around them miserable.

But there are some who face their difficulties and disappointments squarely and do something to change the situation. As I mentioned a moment ago, the difference is their basic internal attitudes.

Over the years we have received hundreds and even thousands of letters in response to various messages presented on our "Herald of Truth" radio and television programs. We appreciate each letter and answer each one personally. These letters help me sound the depth of problems faced by many of our listeners. Often my heart goes out to someone who is facing a discouraging and despairing situation and sees no solution. A few months ago, a mother wrote after listening to one of our messages: "This message had significant value to me. My burdens are heavy and sometimes I feel I just can't go on. I lost my job and have been on welfare since April of this year. I've tried to get a job but can't find one. Vocational rehabilitation is sending me to school in the hopes that I can eventually get a job and support my two children and myself. It is difficult to live on ninety dollars per month when you have two children to feed and clothe. I lead a very lonely life. I get so lonely and depressed, so disheartened about all my problems. I have no people to turn to in times of need. Please pray for me." Needless to say we have prayed for this one whose situation is unusually difficult, not just once, but a number of times. Her loneliness and depression were especially distressing to me.

Another recent letter lingers in my mind. I cannot forget the agony which this mother described and the doubt that sprang from her grief. She wrote, "Who said time heals all wounds? Who said God comforts? Does he walk with me to the cemetery to visit the grave of my six-year-old son who died of leukemia twelve years ago, or the grave of my eighteen-year-old daughter who died of lymphoma two years ago? Does he cry with me? What could he possibly do to ease the pain? Does he know how it hurts to pray to a God who is merciful? Loving? Understanding? I work in a hospital. Does he walk through the corridors to visit the sick, the dying? Is he there to ease the pain, to wipe the tears? No! No! No! . . . I'll feel like this today, and tomorrow and always. Is there really a God, or is he a creation in the mind of man? . . . I'm not satisfied with the answers provided by religion . . . I'd like to meet him face to face and 'tell it like it is'."

What kind of answer can I give to a mother who has suffered the loss of two children and who has come, in bitterness, to doubt the very existence of God? How can I who have never felt the emptiness and loneliness and grief that come with the loss of a child give a meaningful answer to a mother like this? Would not anything I say have a hollow ring? Yet, I believe that there are some answers—some of which I know and some of which others who have suffered the same sort of burden know far better than I.

Who Can Speak?

Not everyone who might wish to do so can bring words of comfort and strength to those who have been bereaved or faced some other crisis. Thomas Carlyle used to say that the chirpy optimism of Ralph Waldo Emerson maddened him because no cloud or shadow had ever darkened Emerson's sheltered life. Emerson appeared to Carlyle like a man who was standing well out of reach of the ocean spray, but who threw out chatty observations on the beauty of the weather to poor souls who were battling for their lives amid the huge billows and dangerous currents of the sea.

There are those, however, who have triumphed over the most difficult situations through faith in God. For at least two thousand years, many who have been overwhelmed by tidal waves of trouble have been inspired by Job, a key book in the Old Testament Scriptures. Perhaps you remember the story. In the opening chapter is this summary of the amazing troubles that befell him suddenly and without warning:

> And it fell on a day when his sons and daughters were eating and drinking wine in their eldest brother's house, that there came a messenger unto Job, and said, The oxen were plowing, and the asses feeding beside them; and the Sabeans fell upon them, and took them away: yea, they have slain the servants with the edge of the sword; and I only am escaped alone to tell thee. While he was yet speaking, there came also another and said, The fire of God is fallen from heaven, and has burned up the sheep and the servants, and consumed them; and I only am escaped alone to tell thee. While he was yet speaking, there came also another, and said, The Chaldeans made three bands, and fell upon the camels, and have taken them away, yea, and slain the servants with the edge of the sword; and I only am escaped alone to tell thee. While he was yet speaking, there came also another, and said, Thy sons and thy daughters were eating and drinking wine in their eldest brother's house; and, behold, there came a great wind from the wilderness, and smote the four corners of the house, and it fell upon the young men, and they are dead: and I only am escaped alone to tell thee. [1:13-19]

In spite of this terrible news, Job responded,

> Naked came I out of my mother's womb, and naked shall I return thither: Jehovah gave, and Jehovah hath taken away; blessed be the name of Jehovah. [1:21]

This is, as many of you will remember, not the end of the story but the beginning. When it was clear that Job had faced his loss of flocks, herds, and possessions, together with the loss of his sons and daughters, without rejecting God, Satan mounted another attack. "So Satan went forth from the presence of Jehovah, and smote Job with sore boils from the sole of his foot unto his crown. And he took him a potsherd to scrape himself therewith; and he sat among the ashes" (2:7, 8). At this point

Job's wife despaired, saying, "Dost thou still hold fast thine integrity? renounce God, and die" (2:9).

A little later in the story Job himself seems, at least momentarily, to be on the brink of despair: "After this opened Job his mouth, and cursed his day. And Job answered and said: Let the day perish wherein I was born, And the night which said, There is a man-child conceived. Let that day be darkness . . . Let darkness and the shadow of death claim it for their own . . . As for that night, let thick darkness seize upon it: Let it not rejoice among the days of the year; Let it not come into the number of the months. Lo, let that night be barren; Let no joyful voice come therein. Let them curse it that curse the day . . ." (3:1-8).

After many days and much contemplation, and after God revealed to Job how little he understood and how weak and powerless he was, Job realized how wise and powerful God is: "Then Job answered Jehovah, and said, I know that thou canst do all things, And that no purpose of thine can be restrained. Who is this that hideth counsel without knowledge? Therefore have I uttered that which I understood not, Things too wonderful for me, which I knew not. Hear, I beseech thee, and I will speak; I will demand of thee, and declare thou unto me. I had heard of thee by the hearing of the ear; But now mine eye seeth thee: Wherefore I abhor myself, And repent in dust and ashes" (42:1-6).

After humbling himself before God, Job was blessed. His greatest triumph came only after he suffered terribly. "Jehovah blessed the latter end of Job more than his beginning: and he had fourteen thousand sheep, and six thousand camels, and a thousand yoke of oxen, and a thousand she-asses. He had also seven sons and three daughters . . . And after this Job lived a hundred and forty years, and saw his sons, and his son's sons, even four generations. So Job died, being old and full of days" (42:12, 13, 16, 17).

No man can fully comprehend the reason for suffering, but the Book of Job offers the most profound advice to be found anywhere: Seek to understand the greatness of God and gladly submit your will to God's, and you will experience peace of mind and blessing. In the history of the world, few people have lost as much as Job did, or have endured as much pain. Yet he faced his disaster without losing faith in God and as a result triumphed over it.

Christ and Paul

When we must carry heavy burdens, we receive our greatest help not from those who, having never carried similar burdens, stand on the sidelines and give bland advice, but from those who have been through the same valleys and have suffered the same problems. In just this way our Lord Jesus Christ has so eminently earned the right to guide us in times of adversity. He spoke from the darkness around the cross. Out of His deep love for mankind, He, the divine Son of God, lived in the squalor of ancient Palestine and then willingly died on the cross for our sins. Betrayed by one of His own followers, condemned by the religious leaders of His day, and forsaken by His most faithful disciples, He suffered the agony of crucifixion. Even in the moment of death He prayed, "Father, forgive them; for they know not what they do" (Luke 23:34).

The apostle Paul described the magnitude of Christ's sacrifice: "Have this mind in you, which was also in Christ Jesus: who, existing in the form of God, counted not the being on an equality with God a thing to be grasped, but emptied himself, taking the form of a servant, being made in the likeness of men; and being found in fashion as a man, he humbled himself, becoming obedient even unto death, yea, the death of the cross." Then, because of His willingness to suffer for mankind, He received the blessings of God, for this same Scripture continues: "Wherefore also God highly exalted him and gave unto him the name which is above every name; that in the name of Jesus every knee should bow, of things in heaven and things on earth and things under the earth, and that every tongue should confess that Jesus Christ is Lord, to the glory of God the Father" (Phil. 2:5-11). No one ever so fully earned the right to help others through adversity. No one can more knowingly guide us when we feel that the burdens of life are too great to bear. The writer of the Hebrew letter adds this further thought: "For we have not a high priest that cannot be touched with the feeling of our infirmities; but one that hath been in all points tempted like as we are, yet without sin. Let us therefore draw near with boldness unto the throne of grace, that we may receive mercy, and may find grace to help us in time of need" (4:15, 16). Christ knows the depths of our suffering because He suffered too.

The apostle Paul also earned the right to speak to those who are suffering. On one occasion he recounted the extent of his suffering: "Of the Jews five times received I forty stripes save one. Thrice was I beaten with rods, once was I stoned, thrice I suffered shipwreck, a night and a day have I been in the deep; in journeyings often, in perils in the wilderness, in perils in the sea, in perils among false brethren; in labor and travail, in watchings often, in hunger and thirst, in fastings often, in cold and nakedness. Besides those things that are without, there is that which presseth upon me daily, anxiety for all the churches" (II Cor. 11:24-28). He gave up a promising career as a young Jewish lawyer in order to suffer this kind of agony for his Lord.

In writing to the young preacher Timothy he could still say, "For which cause I suffer also these things: yet I am not ashamed; for I know him whom I have believed, and I am persuaded that he is able to guard that which I have committed unto him against that day" (II Tim. 1:12). To the Galatians he wrote, "I have been crucified with Christ; and it is no longer I that live, but Christ liveth in me: and that life which I now live in the flesh I live in faith, the faith which is in the Son of God, who loved me, and gave himself up for me" (2:20). It was this same apostle Paul, who had suffered so much, who wrote: "Rejoice in the Lord always: again I will say, Rejoice . . . In nothing be anxious; but in everything by prayer and supplication with thanksgiving let your requests be made known unto God. And the peace of God, which passeth all understanding, shall guard your hearts and your thoughts in Christ Jesus." Then, a moment later, he added, ". . . I have learned, in whatsoever state I am, therein to be content. I know how to be abased, and I know also how to abound: in everything and in all things have I learned the secret both to be filled and to be hungry, both to abound and to be in want. I can do all things in him that strengtheneth me" (Phil. 4:4, 6, 7, 11-13). Out of his suffering, Paul earned the right to point others of us to the way out of darkness when we also suffer.

If ever anyone was justified in despairing, it was this great man who was confined in a Roman prison and ultimately martyred. Yet we find not despair but radiant faith. He knew the Lord intimately and in this relationship, in his complete self-committal to the Lord, found the strength to survive. He who had experienced tribulation, anguish, persecution, famine, naked-ness, peril, and sword nonetheless regarded himself as more than conquerer, saying, "We know that to them that love God all things work together for good, even to them that are called according to his purpose" (Rom. 8:28). At another time Paul wrote, "Yea verily, and I count all things to be loss for the excellency of the knowledge of Christ Jesus my Lord: for whom I suffered the loss of all things, and do count them but refuse, that I may gain Christ" (Phil. 3:8). Out of his suffering he found the greatest blessing of all, a deep and intimate and eternal relationship with the Lord. The great apostle urged the Corinthians, "Be ye imitators of me, even as I also am of Christ" (I Cor. 11:1). In this way we too may find help in time of need.

The Lord Will Help Us, Too

I have faced many situations that were beyond my power to master. I have known the inner shock that comes when the doctor tells a person that he has cancer; suddenly, death seems so close and one's perspective becomes entirely different. I have experienced burdens of the spirit that were even heavier. These inner anxieties are present in the daytime and do not go away at night. Waking or sleeping, I have found them ever-present. Without the strength that comes from Christ and my faith in Him, I could not have survived. Then, too, I have known the emptiness that comes with the death of a member of one's own family.

For many, the most shattering experience of life is the death of a loved one. The bereaved person wanders through life seemingly with no familiar landmarks to guide him. The loss seems so final and so absolute. No formula or theory can take away the immediate, overwhelming pain of bereavement. The Lord does provide a way, however, for us to live with our sorrow and gradually to overcome and forget it.

Norman Vincent Peale tells of

a woman who had a lovely daughter of eighteen who went out riding and was thrown from her horse and killed. The mother had seen her ride away with her cheeks radiant and her spirits high; now she saw her brought back with her eyes closed and her face stilled in death. She could not accept it. And she could not recover from the blow. Deciding to go away to try to forget, she went to a quiet place in the country. But the awful memory went with her. Then as she sat in her room one evening, she took out her Bible and began to read. She read the first Psalm, then one by one, read each of them down to the very last word. She finished and shut the book. She sat quietly, lost in reflection; then she said to herself, with complete conviction: "The men who wrote those Psalms knew about life! They went through suffering just as I am, and they found the answer. And so have I." And at that moment her old stability returned to her; and she was able to pick up her life again. When the minister asked her exactly what the reading of the Psalms had done for her, she replied, "They gave me the answer that I was looking for. And I believed it. The God of those Psalms can be trusted." The Bible had given her the panoramic view, the profound, consoling understanding and the meaning of faith.

I like the words of John Jay, one-time chief justice of the United States Supreme Court: "God is great, and therefore he will be sought; He is good, and therefore He will be found . . . In prosperity, He tries our gratitude; in mediocrity, our contentment; in misfortune, our submission; in darkness, our faith; under temptation, our steadfastness, and at all times our obedience and trust in Him. God governs the world, and we have only to do our duty wisely, and leave the issue to Him."

If you have heavy burdens which sometimes seem too heavy to bear, listen to these words of promise and comfort from the Scripture. David wrote, "O taste and see that Jehovah is good: Blessed is the man that taketh refuge in him. O fear Jehovah, ye his saints; For there is no want to them that fear him" (Ps. 34:8, 9). James wrote, "Every good gift and every perfect gift is from above, coming down from the Father of lights, with whom can be no variation, neither shadow that is cast by turning" (1:17). Jesus said, "Ask, and it shall be given you; seek, and ye shall find; knock, and it shall be opened unto you: for every one that asketh receiveth; and he that seeketh findeth; and to him that knocketh it shall be opened. Or what man is there of you, who, if his son shall ask him for a loaf, will give him a stone; or if he shall ask for a fish, will give him a serpent? If ye then, being evil, know how to give good gifts unto your children, how much more shall your Father who is in heaven give good things to them that ask him?" (Matt. 7:7-11). Jesus further said, "But seek ye first his kingdom, and his righteousness; and all these things shall be added unto you. Be not therefore anxious for the morrow: for the morrow will be anxious for itself. Sufficient unto the day is the evil thereof" (Matt. 6:33, 34). The apostle Peter advised, "Humble yourselves therefore under the mighty hand of God, that he may exalt you in due time; casting all your anxiety upon him, because he careth for you" (I Peter 5:6, 7). With spiritual resources such as these to draw upon, we, too, can face and conquer our frustrations.

4

The Conquest

of Fear

Bertrand Russell once said, "I do not believe that any good thing is to be obtained through fear." Do you agree? Frankly, I would have to take issue with him. Sometimes fear serves a very good purpose; sometimes it even saves lives. For example, we teach our children to fear the dangerous traffic in the streets. Without this fear a child might innocently stray into the street and be crushed under the oncoming wheels of some truck. A child's fear of poison may likewise save his life. When children fear parents they are well behaved. When students fear teachers they are well disciplined. When drivers fear accidents they drive more carefully. When citizens fear law enforcement officers they do not commit crimes. When men fear poverty they work harder and prepare for old age. When people fear health hazards they protect their bodies. They even leave off smoking, drinking, or the use of drugs. When nations fear their enemies they prepare for war. When nations fear atomic destruction they sit down at the peace table. When men fear the judgment they live moral, upright lives. Are there no values in fear? Yes, there are some values precisely because there are some dangers in the world which need to be avoided. Fear helps man avoid that which is harmful and destructive.

Admittedly, however, there is another side to fear. It can have devastating, destructive effects. In the opening paragraphs of his book, *The Conquest of Fear,* Basil King writes: "During most of my conscious life I have been prey to fear . . . I cannot remember the time when a dread of one kind or another was not in the air."

Dominant Emotion of Our World

The dominant emotion of our world is not anger or hate or jealousy, or, on the other hand, love or sympathy, though these emotions obviously are widespread; it is fear. It burdens many people and binds them with invisible chains. John Bonnell points out that "psychologists, by means of laboratory tests, have established that at birth two fears are already present: fear of a loud noise and fear of falling . . . While we begin our lives with only two fears, it is not long before we succeed in accumulating scores of additional ones. The fear of thunder and lightning, of the dark, of people, of life and of death—these have all been taught to children by adults, for they have learned them by watching adult behavior." He continues by saying that sometimes "people are afraid to walk on the streets, afraid to cross a street, afraid to ride in automobiles, or trains, or airplanes . . . And as for imaginary fear, tens of thousands of people throughout this nation are afraid every time they open a letter, tremble when they see the telegraph boy, or are startled when the telephone rings or even when someone suddenly calls to them. They live in constant fear and feel that some strange, indefinable menace haunts all their days."

Dr. George Truett, a noted preacher of the last generation, was invited to speak for a week at one of America's most influential colleges. Thoughtfully, he wrote ahead to the president of the college, asking him to circulate a questionnaire among the students to get their suggestions for subjects and themes for his messages. The most often mentioned request was, "Tell us how we can conquer fear."

All of us have known fear and have known it often. We fear

sicknesses like cancer, tuberculosis, and heart attacks, not to mention the loss of eyesight, hearing, speech, and other faculties. We also fear accidents. Ours is a precarious world in which danger is never far away. We fear insecurity, becoming anxious about getting and keeping a job and about our self-sufficiency in old age. We fear failure. In school, shop, and office, in any human relationships, there is always a possibility of failure. We fear war and destruction which endanger our possessions, our lives, and the lives of our families. We fear death, which hangs over the human race and ultimately comes to all men. The Scriptures speak of those "who through fear of death were all their lifetime subject to bondage" (Heb. 2:15).

The High Cost of Fear

A nationally known psychologist writes, "Fear . . . is often . . . at the bottom of [nervous] breakdowns . . . One reason for the alarming increase in nervous breakdowns and other types of mental illness, is a feeling of emotional insecurity. During World War II approximately two million men and women were either rejected by their examining boards or later discharged, because of mental and nervous ailments." The writer continued, "The general public is . . . becoming so neurotic that one eminent pychiatrist recently said half the American people would be in sanitariums in another generation, with the other half required to wait upon them! While that is probably intended as hyperbole, it does indicate a serious trend." For years it has been widely known that at least half of the hospital beds in our nation are occupied by patients who are mentally ill. One of the chief reasons for their illness is the destructive emotion of fear.

Many of us are disturbed from time to time when we read of a suicide. Approximately twenty thousand people in our nation annually become so depressed and despondent that they take their own lives. In fact, this is the tenth-ranking cause of death today. A person who had attempted suicide unsuccessfully was asked by his physician, "Why did you wish to end your life?" He answered, "I was afraid to go on living." Norman Cousins wrote in *Modern Man Is Obsolete:* "When a man can find no answer he will find fear." In the midst of a confused and sometimes chaotic world, fear is almost inevitable. Some men will feel the burden of fear to such an extent that they will try to escape life altogether.

I have also been impressed with the obvious preoccupation with which modern man contemplates death. The front page of the newspaper on almost any day announces the death of certain prominent people as well as casualty statistics from war, traffic accidents, and accidents of other kinds. Pictures and news stories about death are common, and, of course, obituary pages record the constant march of death. Even Maeterlinck, one of the great minds of this century, said in his autobiography, "I am a frightened child in the presence of death."

The frightened child confides his fears to a father and thereby allays the terrors that have gripped him. The child of God, regardless of his age, is supremely fortunate in that he has a Father in heaven to whom he may take his burdens and fears.

Dr. George W. Crane describes how modern-day pressures produce ulcers, hypertension and other psychosomatic effects. A person finds it difficult to sleep soundly. During the day he may resort to liquor or other drugs and likely is a chain smoker. At night he relies upon sleeping tablets. As a mature adult he now realizes that he is trying to solve his problems all alone. As a result he often grows fearful about his job, his health, and other matters. Quite often he becomes a hypochondriac, who goes from one physician to another, more for sympathy than for medication. In a sense the physicians become glorified parents to millions of patients who crave love and reassurance. The writer continues, "However, if such a man links up with God Almighty in an active partnership, he can throw off his tension at night and, in effect, say a prayer somewhat as follows: 'Oh, heavenly Father we are partners, but now I need sleep, so please take over the night shift for me!' This vivid realization that one has a heavenly Father to fall back upon, will produce remarkable medical benefits. It lessens the tensions, so one's peptic ulcer is not so likely to start gnawing, for the hydrochloric acid secretion is then diminished. Blood pressure will also drop, for fear elevates blood pressure, while peace and confidence reduce it."

The Only Antidote for Fear

Faith in God has always been the only real antidote for fear. I have particularly felt the impact of the words spoken to Joshua when, suddenly after the death of Moses, he was called to lead the ancient Israelitish nation. It was a precarious time for that nation; it had escaped from its Egyptian captors, had wandered over-long in the wilderness, and was ready to settle in the land of Canaan. But first they had to clear the land of its idolatrous inhabitants. The ancient text reads, "Now it came to pass after the death of Moses the servant of Jehovah, that Jehovah spake unto Joshua the son of Nun, Moses' minister, saying . . . Be strong and of good courage; for thou shalt cause this people to inherit the land which I swear unto their fathers to give them . . . Be strong and of good courage; be not affrighted, neither be thou dismayed: for Jehovah thy God is with thee whithersoever thou goest" (Josh. 1:1, 6, 9).

David expressed essentially the same sentiment in his best-known Psalm: "Yea, though I walk through the valley of the shadow of death, I will fear no evil; for thou art with me" (23:4).

In another psalm David wrote, "Though a host should encamp against me, My heart shall not fear: Though war should rise against me, Even then will I be confident" (27:3).

Another psalm contains these comforting words: "God is our refuge and strength, A very present help in trouble. Therefore will we not fear, though the earth do change, And though the mountains be shaken into the heart of the seas" (46:1, 2).

In the New Testament book of Hebrews are these reassuring words: "I will in no wise fail thee, neither will I in any wise forsake thee. So that with good courage we say, The Lord is my helper; I will not fear: What shall man do unto me?" (13:5, 6). The final book of the Bible adds, "Fear not; I am the first and the last, and the Living one; and I was dead, and behold, I am alive for evermore, and I have the keys of death and of Hades" (1:17, 18). The apostle Peter wrote, "Humble yourselves therefore under the mighty hand of God, that he may exalt you in due time; casting all your anxiety upon him, because he careth for you" (I Peter 5:6, 7).

No passage is more comforting, however, than that written by the apostle Paul to the Christians at Rome: "And we know that to them that love God all things work together for good, even to them that are called according to his purpose . . . If God is for us, who is against us? . . . Who shall separate us from the love of Christ? shall tribulation, or anguish, or persecution, or famine, or nakedness, or peril, or sword? . . . Nay, in all these things we are more than conquerors through him that loved us" (8:28, 31, 35, 37). Another passage of encouragement is the fourth chapter of the Book of Philippians, in which Paul says, "In nothing be anxious; but in everything by prayer and supplication with thanksgiving let your requests be made known unto God. And the peace of God, which passeth all understanding, shall guard your hearts and your thoughts in Christ Jesus . . . I have learned, in whatsoever state I am, therein to be content . . . I can do all things in him that strengtheneth me" (vv. 6, 7, 11, 13).

We become calm and confident as we trust the promises of God and follow in the steps of Christ. We have an assurance, a certainty about how to live and how to solve problems. The closer we follow the Lord the less we fear. The wise man Solomon wrote, "The fear of Jehovah is the beginning of wisdom . . ." (Prov. 9:10). Fear of God leads to obedience to His commands. This is not abject fear; it is more akin to reverence and awe. It is not unrelated to the love of God. "There is no fear in love: but perfect love casteth out fear, because fear hath punishment; and he that feareth is not made perfect in love" (I John 4:18). As we learn deeply to love and trust God, fear disappears.

Escape from Fear

Fear has a place, but let us fear only those things that are worthy of fear. Let us balance our fears with vital living faith in God and in His power. Many people are buried under great weights of fear. Their lives are unhappy; they are often broken and distraught. Christ can lift these burdens and give confidence and peace to troubled hearts. In his poem "The Eternal Goodness," John Greenleaf Whittier expresses the Christian's escape from fear:

> I know not where his islands lift
> Their fronded palms in air;
> I only know I cannot drift
> Beyond his love and care.

Then there are these words from a hymn by Isaac Watts:

> Then I can read my title clear
> To mansions in the skies;
> I bid farewell to every fear.
> And wipe my weeping eyes.

"Being therefore justified by faith, we have peace with God through our Lord Jesus Christ" (Rom. 5:1).

"Jesus, Lover of My Soul" was written by Charles Wesley. Later it was set to music and since that time has been sung wherever Christians have gathered to worship God. The second stanza indicates that, if man is to overcome fear, he must have a source of strength beyond himself:

> Other refuge have I none;
> Hangs my helpless soul on Thee;
> Leave, O leave me not alone,
> Still support and comfort me.
> All my trust on Thee is stayed,
> All my help from Thee I bring;
> Cover my defenseless head
> With the shadow of Thy wing.

The prime minister of Japan, speaking from a platform where the flag of Japan would soon stand with the flags of the Allied countries, said, "It is not a treaty of vengeance, but an instrument of reconciliation. The Japanese delegation gladly accepts this fair and generous treaty." The chairman of the conference, Dean Acheson, concluded it with a benediction which had never before been pronounced at such a gathering, but which had been made appropriate by all that had gone before: "I close this conference with words which in many languages, in many forms . . . have brought comfort and strength—'May the peace of God which passeth all understanding be amongst us and remain with us always.' "

God has seen fit to exhort His servants to fear some things and not to fear others. For instance, our Lord said, "I will warn you whom ye shall fear: Fear him, who after he hath killed hath power to cast into hell; yea, I say unto you, Fear him" (Luke 12:5). On the other hand, a follower of Christ is "strengthened with power through his Spirit in the inward man" (Eph. 3:16). He is quite capable of routing the fears that miserably harass unbelievers. The apostle Peter puts the matter in this light: "And who is he that will harm you, if ye be zealous of that which is good? But even if ye should suffer for righteousness' sake, blessed are ye, and fear not their fear, neither be troubled" (I Peter 3:13, 14). There was a time when Jesus' disciples were terrified but the Master said assuringly, "It is I; be not afraid" (John 6:20). When a man has Christ in his heart through faith (Eph. 3:17), he will not be inclined to push the panic button. He possesses strength that surpasses his own. He is fully capable of facing up to life—and death.

George Washington's inaugural address includes these memorable words: "It would be peculiarly improper to omit in this first official act, my fervent supplications to that Almighty Being Who rules over the universe—Who presides in the councils of nations—and Whose providential aids can supply every human defect . . ." How tragic that fear, one of man's great and persistent defects, is not dealt with by the masses in accordance with God's plan for the betterment and the salvation of the races of mankind.

In a day when fear stalks the world's capitals and mass destruction could be triggered at any moment, the hope offered by Christ is the only antidote to fear.

The great Helen Keller once said, "I believe in the immortality of the soul because I have within me immortal longings." A greater than Helen Keller said, ". . . I know him whom I have believed, and I am persuaded that he is able to guard that which I have committed unto him against that day" (II Tim. 1:12). I pray that such confidence and freedom from fear may be yours.

5

The Escape
from Guilt

On the very day that I was completing this chapter, I received in the mail a letter from a young man who had deep guilt feelings. He began his six-page, hand-written letter, "I am twenty-one years old, and am a student at [a state college in the Midwest]. Before finishing his opening paragraph he mentioned "the problem that I have." In his second paragraph he said, "I have finally come to the point where I now realize that running away from a problem does not solve it . . . my past life has been sin filled, with extremely degrading sins. Not only has this caused fear to be present, but I also feel at times that I could not possibly be forgiven." On the second page of his letter he wrote, "At certain times the whole matter would seem absolutely hopeless, and at other times some hope would come. At one point I was close to suicide—or at least the thought entered my mind more than once." On the third page he added, "I now realize what a horrible predicament I am in . . . But it is hard for me to accept the fact that my life is through at twenty-one." Still later in his letter he said, "What I want more than anything now is just to do what really is the right thing and in the right way." This young man was carrying a heavy burden of guilt.

At the end of a recent school year I received an unsigned note from one of my students: "You don't know me so my name is not important. I am a graduating senior and I have been in your classes two different quarters since I have been here. I want to thank you and let you know that I got a lot out of those two quarters of the study of the Bible. I have a favor to ask of you—I made a mistake this quarter, and if you would, please pray that I can make up for this mistake . . . It would be just a little mistake to most people, but it is about to drive me crazy. Thank you very much." This student, too, felt the burden of guilt which always follows sin.

Inevitability of Guilt

The Bible is full of examples of men and women who disregarded God in order to go their own willful ways. Over and over again we note their ultimate feelings of failure and guilt. For example, Israel's first king was the fine, capable young man Saul. Later, after he had grown older and been influenced by the world about him, he was overwhelmed by feelings of jealousy and resentment against David. Ultimately he despaired and committed suicide on Mount Gilboa.

David, his successor on the throne, in his later years fell into serious sin. He verbalized his guilt feelings in the fifty-first Psalm: "For I know my transgressions; and my sin is ever before me. Against thee, thee only, have I sinned and done that which is evil in thy sight . . . Create in me a clean heart, O God; and renew a right spirit within me. Cast me not away from thy presence; and take not thy holy Spirit from me. Restore unto me the joy of thy salvation; and uphold me with a willing spirit . . . Deliver me from bloodguiltiness, O God, thou God of my salvation; And my tongue shall sing aloud of thy righteousness" (vv. 3, 4, 10-12, 14).

David was followed by Solomon, who began well but drifted into idolatry, materialism, and sensualism. It was he who penned the lines, "But the way of the transgressor is hard" (Prov. 13:15).

The prophet Isaiah obviously felt unworthy when he wrote, "Woe is me! for I am undone; because I am a man of unclean lips, and I dwell in the midst of a people of unclean lips: for mine eyes have seen the King, Jehovah of hosts" (6:5).

Simon Peter, when he was with Jesus at the Sea of Galilee, "fell down at Jesus' knees, saying, Depart from me; for I am a sinful man, O Lord" (Luke 5:8). Notice his feeling of unworthiness. We are all familiar with Judas, who "when he saw that he was condemned, repented himself, and brought back the thirty pieces of silver to the chief priests and elders, saying, I have sinned in that I betrayed innocent blood. But they said, What is that to us? see thou to it. And he cast down the pieces of silver into the sanctuary and departed; and he went away and hanged himself" (Matt. 27:3-5). He was overwhelmed with remorse and guilt.

The fact that Jesus is a friend of sinners (Luke 5:32; I Tim. 1:15) should sustain guilt-ridden souls the world over. Christ is our Savior. His offer of salvation from sin is unique. He, above all others, is our friend.

To Feel Guilt Is a Blessing

God created man with a capacity to feel guilt. Each of us has a conscience, an inner sense of right and wrong, a kind of governor for our actions. It causes us to feel the burden of guilt after committing sin. Modern psychologists and psychiatrists often look upon feelings of guilt as interlopers, but they shouldn't. If one seeks relief from them properly, he can profit from them. But if one seeks merely to escape or quench them, he can expect difficulty and, in some instances, disaster.

Feelings of guilt may be uncomfortable but they are a kind of distress or warning signal, such as those which warn the railroad engineer of danger ahead. The conscience is comparable to our physical capacities to feel pain. Thoughtful people recognize the pain endings all over our bodies as a blessing, not because they enjoy pain or look forward to the physical injury, but because they are grateful for a system of warning in which lesser pains protect us from greater ones.

Some years ago Robert Wadlow, the world's tallest man, died

at an early age from an infection in his heel. He had no pain endings in his heel, so a blister appeared on it and became infected without his knowing about it. Antibiotic wonder drugs hadn't yet been developed, so the infection proved fatal. If he had had the normal pain endings in his heel, he would have been warned early enough to save his life.

When you inadvertently put your hand on a hot stove, immediately you feel the pain and instinctively pull the hand back. That pain keeps you from burning the hand irreparably and possibly losing it entirely. In similar fashion, when we feel pangs of guilt, we are warned against spiritual danger.

The famous author Truman Capote told in his well-known best seller, *In Cold Blood,* about some young ruffians who murdered the Clutter family in cold blood—for no reason, just for the "kicks." And they felt no remorse. There was no pity, no sorrow, no regret. In fact, as they left the scene of the crime, they were roaring with laughter. The apostle Paul speaks of such people as being "past feeling."

In Ephesians 4:18, 19, he says such people are "darkened in their understanding, alienated from the life of God, because of the ignorance that is in them, because of the hardening of their heart . . . being past feeling [they] gave themselves up to lasciviousness, to work all uncleanness with greediness."

Not To Feel Guilt

One of the tragedies of our day is that many people do not feel guilt. Their consciences have been untrained or mistrained and they do not understand the seriousness of sin. They consider sin a mistake, or poor judgment, or a result of wrong influences. Man's responsibility for wrong doing is explained away. Sin and judgment and hell are considered obsolete and the words are being dropped from modern man's vocabulary. But sin is not imaginary; it is real. In fact, the consequences of man's sin are so great that it was necessary for Christ to come to the earth and to die for our sins. Knowing the awful tragedy of unforgiven sin, God loved the world enough to send "his only begotten Son, that whosoever believeth on him should not perish, but have eternal life" (John 3:16).

The apostle John defined sin as lawlessness: "Every one that doeth sin doeth also lawlessness; and sin is lawlessness" (I John 3:4). The transgression of God's law is sin, whether by omission or commission, whether in thought, word, or deed. The Bible includes all sins in one of three categories: the lust of the flesh, the lust of the eye, and the pride of life (I John 2:16).

In the same epistle of John we read: "If we say that we have no sin, we deceive ourselves, and the truth is not in us . . . If we say that we have not sinned, we make him a liar; and his word is not in us" (1:8, 10). The apostle Paul had written earlier, "There is none righteous, no, not one . . . all have sinned, and fall short of the glory of God" (Rom. 3:10, 23). With the exception of the sinless Son of God, all men have been contaminated with sin.

Either consciously or unconsciously man feels the effects of his sins. As Solomon said, "The way of the transgressor is hard." No sin lacks consequences. I knew a man some years ago who in his later years was deeply troubled by the careless behavior of his youth. On several different occasions he talked with me about things he did at least forty years before. I tried to assure him that his Christian profession and his long, faithful, Christian life removed all guilt, but without success. He had so long dwelt upon these misdeeds in his subconscious mind that they were disturbing him very deeply. He would go home, only to come back again within a few days. He even spent time in a mental hospital. But the burden of guilt stayed with him to the very end of his life. Many a person does not realize how deeply sin scars his soul and how much suffering it will bring in the years to come.

Young people—and others—who disregard God's way of life do not yet know the extent of its costs. All sin has its consequences. "The way of the transgressor is hard."

The greatness of David, a man after God's heart, lay in a recognition of his own weakness and of his constant need for God: "I will lift up mine eyes unto the mountains: From whence shall my help come? My help cometh from Jehovah, Who made heaven and earth" (Ps. 121:1, 2).

While John the Baptist, the forerunner of the Lord, was standing at the banks of the Jordan, he saw Jesus coming in the distance and said, "Behold, the Lamb of God, that taketh away the sin of the world!" (John 1:29). Jesus does for man what man is not able to do for himself.

Since God expelled Adam and Eve from the garden of Eden, humanity has borne this great burden of sin. The ancient Hebrew tradition requires the chief priest on the annual Day of Atonement to take a goat, called the scapegoat, and then (symbolically) place upon it the sins of the people and send it out into the wilderness. But, of course, it didn't really take away their sins. It did, in a sense, roll them forward for another year.

In Hebrews 10:4 we read, "For it is impossible that the blood of bulls and goats should take away sins." No, only the Lord Jesus Christ can take away the sins of mankind. This was affirmed by the apostles. The apostle Paul in Romans 3:24, 25 says that Christians are "justified freely by his grace through the redemption that is in Christ Jesus: whom God set forth to be a propitiation, through faith, in his blood . . ." And that word *propitiation* means simply "atonement." And so He is our atonement, through faith in His blood. Christ came to earth to take away from man the burden of guilt for man's sins.

The One Who Bears Our Guilt

Some time ago a friend of mine was vacationing on Tybee Island near Savannah, Georgia. He and his little son were fishing in an inlet. The tide was running rather swiftly and this little boy stood up in the boat, lost his balance, and fell into these swiftly moving currents. The father immediately dived in after his son, and both drowned. The father loved his son more than he loved his own life. Men will give their lives for those whom they love. Our Lord gave His life even for His enemies.

Charles Dickens' famous *Tale of Two Cities* tells about Charles Darnay, a young Frenchman who was condemned to the guillotine. But a second young man, a dissolute young British lawyer who is, nevertheless, a friend of Darnay, comes to the condemned man's rescue. On the night before the execution Sidney Carton presents himself at the gate of the prison and is allowed to enter. He goes to the dungeon and there exchanges clothes with Darnay. Darnay goes free; Carton dies on the guillotine.

Of all of the Old Testament prophecies of the Messiah, the most meaningful is found in Isaiah 53:

> But he was wounded for our transgressions, he was bruised for our iniquities; the chastisement of our peace was upon him; and with his stripes we are healed. . . . He was oppressed, yet when he was afflicted he opened not his mouth; as a lamb that is led to the slaughter, and as a sheep that before its shearers is dumb, so he opened not his mouth . . . And they made his grave with the wicked, and with a rich man in his death; although he had done no violence, neither was any deceit in his mouth . . . Therefore will I divide him a portion with the great, and he shall divide the spoil with the strong; because he poured out his soul unto death, and was numbered with the transgressors: he bare the sin of many, and made intercession for the transgressors. [vv. 5, 7, 9, 12]

Thomas Chalmers, the British preacher, made this passage even more meaningful by personalizing it. After his death, a friend who was examining his effects looked at his Bible, the Bible from which he had preached, the Bible that he had studied for a lifetime. And in Isaiah 53 he found that Chalmers had marked through the plural pronouns and had penciled in the singular: ". . . he was wounded for MY transgressions, he was bruised for MY iniquity; the chastisement of MY peace was upon him; and with his stripes I am healed."

Some seven hundred years after Isaiah prophesied, Jesus gave His life for the sins of all mankind. The sinless Son of Man, the glorious Son of God, was crucified on Calvary; and even in the hour of death He prayed, "Father, forgive them; for they know not what they do," for those who had mocked Him; who'd spat upon Him; and who crucified Him.

On the night of His crucifixion, Jesus was betrayed by Judas Iscariot. Afterward Judas said, "I have sinned in that I have betrayed innocent blood." Then the Scripture adds, "And he went away and hanged himself." When some people realize the seriousness of their sins, they simply despair. Many down through the centuries have taken their own lives when they realized just how guilty they were. This reaction is not only wrong, it is unnecessary.

The Right Way

On that same night that the Lord was betrayed, He was denied by Peter. Luke tells us that after Peter had denied his Lord the third time, "he went out, and wept bitterly" (Luke 22:62). However, this is not the end of the story. Seven weeks later at Pentecost, after Peter had deeply repented of his sin, he preached one of the world's greatest sermons. Through the years that followed he faithfully served his Lord, a living demonstration that sin of even the worst kind can be overcome and the burden of guilt removed. This is the avenue which Christ came to open for those who would accept it.

Peter later preached to others: ". . . ye were redeemed, not with corruptible things, with silver or gold, from your vain manner of life handed down from your fathers; but with precious blood, as of a lamb without blemish and without spot, even the blood of Christ: who was foreknown indeed before the foundation of the world, but was manifested at the end of the times for your sake, who through him are believers in God, that raised him from the dead, and gave him glory; so that your faith and hope might be in God" (I Peter 1:18-21). The transforming power of the gospel, lifting the guilty from the hopelessness of sin, is seen in every genuine Christian. In the words of Paul, "Be not fashioned according to this world: but be ye transformed by the renewing of your mind, that ye may prove what is the good and acceptable and perfect will of God" (Rom. 12:2). How very appropriate are the words of the familiar hymn:

> Could my tears forever flow,
> Could my zeal no languor know,
> These for sin could not atone;
> Thou must save, and Thou alone:
> In my hand no price I bring,
> Simply to Thy cross I cling.

Five Simple Suggestions

Someone asks, "How can I get rid of my guilt? Tell me how to do it." Let me make five simple but significant suggestions.

Take God at His word. He has promised to forgive us if we will forgive others. In Matthew 6:14, 15, Jesus said, "For if ye forgive men their trespasses, your heavenly Father will also forgive you. But if ye forgive not men their trespasses, neither will your Father forgive your trespasses."

Admit to God that you have done wrong and that you are genuinely sorry. This is repentance and it also involves making right everything you can, relative to your sins.

Forgive everyone who has wronged you. Genuinely remove the hatred, resentment, and jealousy which you may feel toward anyone else by honestly forgiving them completely.

Sincerely, one time and one time only, ask God to forgive you. This prayer should be earnest and deep and genuine. But then, do not follow the common practice of praying it over and over and over again through the years. Do not repeat this prayer forever.

Finally, *accept the forgiveness which God has promised to give you.* When the thought of your sin comes back to your mind, instead of praying, "Father, forgive me for my sin . . . ," pray instead, "I thank thee, Father, for forgiving me." He has promised to forgive. We must believe that He has kept His promise. Instead of deepening our feeling of guilt through the years by repeating the request for forgiveness, we turn our attention time and again to God's goodness in forgiving us. One of these attitudes burdens and destroys, the other lifts and inspires. Rather than the negative, destructive attitude, let us have the positive, constructive, Christian attitude, believing that God has forgiven us.

God has invited man to come to Him for pardon in whatever situation man finds himself. No situations are hopeless and impossible. God is always willing to forgive anything if only man will respond to His loving direction. Those who have never come to Christ need to believe in the Lord as the Savior of the world, repent of their sins, and then become obedient to the

Lord's commands to confess their faith in Christ before men and to be buried with Him in baptism for the remission of their sins (Acts 2:38). The blood of Christ cleanses the sinner, as mentioned by the apostle John: "If we walk in the light, as he is in the light, we have fellowship one with another, and the blood of Jesus his Son cleanseth us from all sin" (I John 1:7).

Sometimes, however, the sinner is already a Christian. What should he do? He should repent and pray for forgiveness. The apostle Peter gave these words of admonition to Simon, a young Christian: "Repent therefore of this thy wickedness, and pray the Lord, if perhaps the thought of thy heart shall be forgiven thee" (Acts 8:22).

To needlessly bear the burden of guilt for sin is a great tragedy. Christ came to earth to lift that burden from you. The Lord lived and died in order to cleanse you and make you free. This is the good news of Jesus Christ.

6

The Reality
of Pain

Pain is everywhere. At times it comes with the suddenness of a lightning flash. At other times it comes gradually and is scarcely noticed until it begins to mount throbbingly, insistently, to a degree and intensity that cannot be ignored. Pain may be self-induced or it may result from carelessness. Just as often it comes to the innocent. It is seldom announced; it is always unwanted. Pain is part of daily living. Man enters this world with a cry of pain—and leaves with a sigh.

At various times each of us has felt severe physical pain. Sometimes it was almost overwhelming. Disease brings excruciating pain to sufferers the world over. Accidents bring pain: a fall and broken bones . . . a severe burn . . . an automobile crash that cuts and mangles the body. Starvation and thirst are painful, as is the torture used by tyrants to break the will of an enemy. But any of these physical pains may be easier to bear than the pain of the mind and spirit.

Is there some reason for man's pain? Does it serve some good purpose? Is there an adequate explanation for it? The problem of human suffering is one of the most puzzling. Why must there be disease and death? Especially, why must the innocent, such as children, suffer?

Although he himself was a believer in Christ and a defender of Christianity, C. S. Lewis included in his fine book, *The Problem of Pain,* the critic's question, "If God were good, He would wish to make His creatures perfectly happy, and if God were almighty, He would be able to do what He wished. But the creatures are not happy. Therefore God lacks either goodness, or power, or both." Is there an answer to this question?

A Result of Man's Sin

God created man with a free will, which allowed man to choose evil as well as good. The only alternative was to create an automaton which did good because that's all it was capable of doing. By making man free, his good acts have real significance. It also results in mistakes, blunders, and wrong choices. The events of history give ample evidence that man has often chosen wrongly and has suffered as a result.

Suffering often results from man's own sin. The man who drinks heavily eventually pays the price in his own body and in the tangled strands of his own life. The person who misuses his body in any way will eventually pay the price. The liar, the cheat, the hypocrite also inevitably suffer.

But not all suffering is the result of man's sin. Our Lord Himself made this plain. "Now there were some present at that very season who told him of the Galileans, whose blood Pilate had mingled with their sacrifices. And he answered and said unto them, Think ye that these Galileans were sinners above all the Galileans, because they have suffered these things? I tell you, Nay: but except ye repent, ye shall all in like manner perish" (Luke 13:1-3). Pilate's victims were not any more wicked than the rest.

Jesus addressed the same subject on another occasion. "And as he passed by, he saw a man blind from his birth. And his disciples asked him, saying, Rabbi, who sinned, this man, or his parents, that he should be born blind? Jesus answered, Neither did this man sin, nor his parents: but that the works of God should be made manifest in him" (John 9:1-3). Taking Christ as our final authority, we reject the idea that one's sin explains all of his suffering. Much suffering comes to the innocent.

Men also suffer because they live together—"For none of us liveth to himself, and none dieth to himself" (Rom. 14:7)—and because the iniquity of the fathers affects their children even to the third and fourth generation (Exod. 20:5). The nature of the universe is such that when certain causes are put into operation certain effects inevitably follow. Sin, which is essentially rebellion against the will of God, inevitably causes suffering.

Sometimes the sin of a drunken driver on the highway must be paid for in part by innocent travelers who have never met the sinner before. Life together upon the earth does result in the innocent suffering, but it is also the source of the most cherished blessings available to mankind.

The Nature of the Universe

The nature of the universe helps to explain human suffering. The universe is a system of law and order, a system in which everything is *faithful*. Scientific investigations made in one part of the world can be verified through the same experiments in another. The natural laws of our universe are uniform. If they weren't, our world could not operate. Principles true today must be true tomorrow.

This uniformity, this system of law and order, also has much to do with man's suffering. Take fire, for example. The natural laws of the universe which God created enable man, if he uses the right elements and the right processes, to create fire. The same law that enables us to have fire for cooking our meals and heating our homes also enables us to have fire which will burn our houses and destroy our lives. The law that made it possible to have fire for constructive purposes may be misused for destructive purposes.

One of man's greatest achievements is the automobile, but along with its fine uses there are tragic ones. Similarly, steel which makes possible great buildings can also be used for guns and tanks which destroy lives in war. The principles of nature, if used properly, result in good. If used improperly, they carry the power of destruction.

But this is not the whole story. When God created the universe with its natural laws, He established the system by which the seas provide moisture for the continents. As temperature changes cause rainfall, and as the water falls gently upon the fields, God is providing the means for all life to exist. However, in this same process, the rain will sometimes cause houses to be torn from their foundations and lives to be lost. The whole process of nature has an occasional by-product or side effect—a storm. This further explains man's suffering. Consequently, it becomes increasingly imperative that we look beyond immediate concerns, no matter how serious or critical, to the master plan —God's plan—for the human race.

Is Suffering Always Evil?

Man generally assumes that all human suffering is evil. Let us examine this presupposition to see if it is true. Is the negative value which we ascribe to suffering its real value? Man's primary purpose is to honor and glorify God, and to become as Godlike as is humanly possible. Therefore, evil is that which takes him away from God, and good is that which brings man toward God.

Once we accept this standard, we can see the events of our world in a different light. It is quite possible that the riches, honors, and pleasures of the world hinder rather than help. It is quite conceivable that illness, loss of money, and even the loss of friends might ultimately serve some good purpose. Under certain circumstances poverty is better than riches. We know that Jesus said, "A man's life consisteth not in the abundance of the things which he possesseth" (Luke 12:15). All too often the material things of our world blind us to the spiritual things and thus become curses instead of blessings, not just for a time, but for eternity. Riches, honors, and pleasures are not necessarily evil; they can also be blessings. It depends on our attitude toward them; it depends on how we use them. Do they draw us closer to God or pry us away from God? No one would claim that suffering is good in itself, but it is good when it brings us into submission to God's will.

Often Beneficial

Suffering is often beneficial. Much of the pain that we suffer is remedial in character. Part of sin's deceitfulness is that, as long as things are well with us, we have little disposition to give up error and sin. Only when we are hurt do we feel a need for God. It is by suffering that we overcome. A man who has no sorrow in his life is immature. It is through hard work that we develop spiritual strength, strength to overcome the lust of the flesh, the lust of the eye, and the pride of life.

Things that looked so glamorous before, after a period of crisis in which we come face-to-face with the real issues of life, look like tinsel and glitter, mere baubles on a Christmas tree.

Some people live as if the chief end of their lives is their own happiness—a freedom from pain or suffering or anything unpleasant. The worst thing about such a notion is that it removes God from the center of things. It ignores the possibility that pain is God's method of bringing us back to Him. As a father loves his child and corrects him and disciplines him for his own good, so God lets His children suffer that they may have the greater blessings which both life and eternity have to offer. In the Letter to the Hebrews we read, "For whom the Lord loveth he chasteneth, and scourgeth every son whom he receiveth. It is for chastening that ye endure; God dealeth with you as with sons; for what son is there whom his father chasteneth not?" (12:6, 7). This is what the psalmist meant when he said, "It is good for me that I have been afflicted; that I may learn thy statutes (Ps. 119:71).

Suffering Builds Character

Suffering also has the power to ennoble the character and spirit of the sufferer. Some people seem to feel that the love of God guarantees them everything they wish. Their expectation is unreasonable because God's love for man is never described in the Scriptures as soft, indulgent, and humoring. God is a potter who carefully and painstakingly forms from the shapeless clay a vessel of honor. He is a builder who carefully cuts and places stones to make a beautiful edifice. He is a shepherd who devotedly cares for, but also guides and restricts, his flock to keep them safe. He is a father who disciplines and corrects every son whom he receives; a father who genuinely loves his child must from time to time discipline that child, which causes the child to suffer but also protects him from greater suffering and even from destroying himself. Loving care involves discipline.

If God promised immunity from suffering to those who follow Him, men would serve Him out of self-interest, and they would never develop the beauty and strength of character for which all should strive. No, God does not promise that His children will be immune to all suffering, but He does promise ". . . to them that love God all things work together for good, even to them that are called according to his purpose" (Rom. 8:28).

Battered by his enemies and distressed by intrigues, King David looked beyond his immediate suffering to the majesty of God's mercy. It is particularly fitting that the last words of the last Psalm should urge "everything that hath breath" to "praise Jehovah" (150:6).

Look Up—Toward Heaven

The Bible describes man's existence on the earth as a temporary sojourn during which man is prepared for a better and a more permanent abode in heaven. We read that Abraham "looked for the city which hath the foundations, whose builder and maker is God" (Heb. 11:10). In the same chapter we also read that Moses chose to live and work among God's people rather than to enjoy the pleasures of Egypt, "for he looked unto the recompense of reward" (v. 26). At other times Paul said that "our citizenship is in heaven" (Phil 3:20), and that, "though our outward man is decaying, yet our inward man is renewed day by day. For our light affliction which is for the moment, worketh for us more and more exceedingly an eternal weight of glory . . . For we know that if the earthly house of our tabernacle be dissolved, we have a building from God, a house not made with hands, eternal, in the heavens" (II Cor. 4:16, 17; 5:1). To the Romans Paul wrote "that the sufferings of this present time are not worthy to be compared with the glory which shall be revealed to usward" (8:18).

God has prepared for us a home and to that home He wishes us to come. Were it not for the heartaches, disappointments, and sufferings of this world we might forget the greater destiny that lies before us. The sufferings of this world were designed, in part, to prevent us from being satisfied here and to direct our eyes toward the more wonderful world to come.

The greatest need of pain-ridden, suffering mankind is the healing ministry of the Great Physician, our Lord Jesus Christ. It is not enough for a man merely to get things off his chest on the psychologist's or psychiatrist's couch. Christ alone can relieve us of the pain and misery of sin. Christ alone offers the hope of salvation. He calls us by His gospel (II Thess. 2:14) to faithfulness and obedience. The wise man of God enunciated the ancient, unchanging principle—"He that covereth his transgressions shall not prosper; But whoso confesseth and forsaketh them shall obtain mercy" (Prov. 28:13). Christ is the way of life, the only way (John 14:6). Christ is the one mediator between God and man (I Tim. 2:5). There is no other. When we think of the suffering to which fallen mankind is heir, we would do well to think of the suffering of Christ who died that we might live completely free of suffering—forever. In the words of Isaiah, "He was wounded for our transgressions, he was bruised for our iniquities; the chastisement of our peace was upon him; and with his stripes we are healed" (53:5).

Pain is here to stay—for the duration of our lives on earth. Since this is undeniably true, why not use it to our own advantage, by attending faithfully to the inspired word of God which is able to save our souls (James 1:21)? From that holy, inspired word I leave with you this imperishable truth:

> Blessed be the God and Father of our Lord Jesus Christ, who according to his great mercy begat us again unto a living hope by the resurrection of Jesus Christ from the dead, unto an inheritance incorruptible, and undefiled, and that fadeth not away, reserved in heaven for you, who by the power of God are guarded through faith unto a salvation ready to be revealed in the last time. Wherein ye greatly rejoice, though now for a little while, if need be, ye have been put to grief in manifold trials, that the proof of your faith, being more precious than gold that perisheth though it is proved by fire, may be found unto praise and glory

and honor at the revelation of Jesus Christ: whom not having
seen ye love; on whom, though now ye see him not, yet believing,
ye rejoice greatly with joy unspeakable and full of glory: receiving the end of your faith, even the salvation of your souls.
[I Peter 1:3-9]

7

The Blight
of Alcohol

A distraught wife and mother who listens to the "Herald of Truth" radio and television programs recently wrote to me: "I heard your broadcast regarding alcoholism and I sat and cried . . . My three children and I have lived with alcoholism and the human toll is so horrible that the financial toll is nothing in comparison." How many marriages have been blighted by the curse of alcohol? How many thousands of children have been deprived of many of life's necessities—adequate food, clothing, housing, and parents whom they can love, respect, and admire—by the curse of alcohol? Can anything be done for a family with an alcoholic father, mother, son, or daughter? Yes, I believe it can.

What We've Said Before

Half a dozen years ago I said on "Herald of Truth":

There are five million alcoholics in the United States. This means, of course, that alcoholism has reached epidemic proportions. All efforts to curb the raging menace of alcoholism have met with unflagging resistance. The monster's giant strides continue unabated. It is reliably reported that loss to industry alone exceeds

70

one billion dollars each year. However, monetary loss is slight when compared to the blighted lives of millions. Drinking has shattered the hopes and dreams of persons in every walk of life. The plans of men and women for a better tomorrow have ended in today's blind alley of utter hopelessness. The total number adversely affected, directly and indirectly, by the five million alcoholics in our land is almost incalculable. What a price to pay for the dubious pleasure of drinking!

Were I giving that same message today, I would need to say, "More than six million people in the United States are alcoholics, and at least another six million are problem drinkers, dangerously close to slipping over into the category of the alcoholic. In fact, a half-million people are becoming alcoholics each year in our nation alone."

In addition to the self-inflicted suffering of the heavy drinker himself is that which he inflicts on three or four others, close relatives and friends. Industry loses two billion dollars annually, according to an article in the Wall Street Journal, which quoted statistics from the National Council on Alcoholism. More serious still, alcohol morally and spiritually devastates millions of people today. Also, of the more than fifty thousand deaths on our highways each year, the National Safety Council and the American Medical Association indicate that approximately half involve drinking drivers. The Department of Health, Education and Welfare now places alcoholism fourth on the list of public health menaces, preceded only by heart disease, mental illness, and cancer.

Worse Than Cigarettes

During the past decade the Surgeon General of the United States and many other responsible sources who are in a position to know the facts have testified to the harmful effects of cigarette smoking upon physical health. Statistics now clearly demonstrate the vast damage to the circulatory system that results from long, continued smoking. The development of emphysema is also frighteningly common. In addition, there are the devastating effects of cancer of the lungs, of the throat, and of the mouth. As a result of this increased knowledge, we have outlawed the advertising of cigarettes on radio and television and have forced the industry to print on each package of cigarettes a statement that smoking can be harmful to physical health.

In my judgment, this is good; people need to be warned and hopefully saved from the tragic results of this unnecessary, expensive, and damaging habit. However, I consider the drinking of alcoholic beverages to be far more damaging to physical health than cigarette smoking could ever be. It also has many other frighteningly serious results, some of which we have mentioned already. Why have we not outlawed the advertising on radio and television of liquor? What inconsistencies there are in our national attitude! If the public needs to be warned against the harmful effects of smoking cigarettes—and it does, does it not need infinitely more to be warned against the damaging effects of alcohol?

An Insidious Evil

Over the years young people in college and those whom I have counseled in private have occasionally asked me the question, in one form or another, "What about social drinking?" The practice of having a cocktail before meals, and at other times, has increased tremendously in recent years, to the point that in business and industry almost all functions are accompanied by liquor. You can hardly travel by air without attractive stewardesses giving numerous offers of a cocktail. You can hardly attend a convention without being encouraged repeatedly to visit the hospitality room. You can hardly attend a formal dinner without being invited to come early for the "hospitality" hour. In addition to the millions who make a cocktail before an evening meal their standard practice are vast numbers who also indulge in the lunchtime cocktail, making a man unable to do his afternoon work in a normal manner. "What about this growing practice?" I am constantly asked. The only answer I can give, the only honest appraisal I can make, is that this is a long stride in the wrong direction, away from health and morality and the ultimate happiness of America.

When I talk with people about social drinking I feel impelled to mention that one out of every thirteen social drinkers ultimately becomes an alcoholic. No one can know when he begins whether he has this special susceptibility to alcohol that will make him the one in thirteen who will ultimately be ruined by it. Drinking socially or in any other way is too dangerous to begin. Experts tell us that ninety-nine out of one hundred alcoholics began as social drinkers and that each year, in the United States alone, approximately half a million people who have been social drinkers will cross over the line into alcoholism. This is too great a risk to run. The only safe course is not to begin at all.

Thirteen Steps

Some time ago I read "Thirteen Steps to Alcoholism," written by a knowledgeable but anonymous observer. Here is an abridged version of these thirteen steps to spiritual oblivion:

No. 1: You drink socially. You start taking a cocktail now and then. Undeniable statistics show that one out of every thirteen in this group will become an alcoholic.

No. 2: "Blackouts" begin. Getting "high" with some regularity, you find yourself going with the crowd that likes to drink heavily. Then one "morning after" you can't recall what you did after a certain point. You have a temporary loss of memory, a danger sign on the road to alcoholism.

No. 3: Liquor now means more to you. Sipping changes to gulping. You are now after the "kick," not sociability. You begin to feel vaguely uneasy about your drinking.

No. 4: You lose control. You can still control whether you will drink tomorrow or next week, but once you do take a drink you can no longer control how many you will take. This is a critical point; if you can see the red light and stop, you may yet save yourself.

No. 5: Your alibi system. If you don't heed the warning in your loss of control, you will start making elaborate excuses for it. The excuses fool no one except you.

No. 6: Morning "eye openers." You now need a stiff drink to help you face a new day. A drink steadies your nerves—nerves that have been made unsteady by drinking. The morning drink eases your conscience, lifts your ego, and *increases your dependence on alcohol!*

No. 7: You drink alone. Solitary drinking offers a quick way into a world of make-believe where you can tell off the boss, amaze your friends with your brilliance, and perform fantastic feats. You are now in serious trouble, but woe unto that one who tries to tell you so!

No. 8: Drinking becomes anti-social. You are not now merely staying away from friends and drinking alone, but often you become destructive—you damage property and hurt people including your own family. Next day you may be horrified at the thought of what you did. You have a growing sense of inadequacy and incompetence. Your only answer—you think—is a drink.

No. 9: Real drinking bouts begin. You now engage in what is termed "a bender," during which you drink blindly, helplessly, with just one goal: to get drunk. There remain just two things —you and liquor; no more concern for family, friends, job, or even food and shelter.

No. 10: Remorse and Resentment. On one hand you see yourself as a failure, a wrecker of lives nearest and dearest to you—and often you feel so guilty your only recourse is another bender! But working against your self-condemnation is a deep-seated belief that your drinking is blameless, that you have good reasons for it, that nobody tries to understand how innocent you are, and besides, the world is against you. This calls for another drink.

No. 11: A deep, nameless anxiety. You begin to feel a vague but ever-present fear. Your hands tremble, your stare is vacant, your step is unsure and your nerves are agonizingly jumpy. Literally and figuratively you have "the shakes."

No. 12: You know you're licked. The day comes when, for the first time, you admit to yourself that you are helpless. You may have a horrible case of delirium tremens. Pink elephants and other monstrosities are no laughing matter; they are frighteningly real. Your excuses no longer satisfy even you.

No. 13: You must get help or else! Now, usually at the end of twelve or fifteen years of deterioration from constant drinking, you are a shambling, haggard, twitching shell of your former self. You have thrown away love, respect, and friendship. You have lost your job, your home, and your future. You have now reached bottom. *But you can live: You can come back—if you will!"*

Alcoholism

What a tragic picture this is and how common it is becoming. Dr. Mark Keller, editor of the *Quarterly Journal of the Studies of Alcohol,* gave this definition: "Alcoholism is a disease, a condition of illness or unhealth, characterized by a form of behavior which the alcoholic cannot control, that of drinking alcoholic beverages in an amount that seems wrong to others and creates injury to health, economic welfare or personal relationships." Let us add this bit of wisdom as a footnote: "Alcoholism is the only disease that requires a license to propagate it. It is the only disease that is bottled and sold; that is spread by advertising; that is a habit-forming; and—it's the only disease that bars the patient from heaven!"

Recently one of the local doctors in my home city, who has dealt with alcoholics for years, wrote,

> Chronic alcoholism results in alcoholic deterioration of the brain —a type of mental illness that affects many alcoholics who fail to overcome their habit while managing somehow to live beyond middle age. After years of continuous or periodic drinking, such people experience a slow but growing personality change, always of an adverse nature. During these years, the victim will often have attacks of delirium tremens, acute hallucinosis and alcoholic polyneuritis. This overall alcoholic deterioration usually involves not only temperament and ability to get along with others, but often is accompanied by dangerous devaluation of the drinker's moral and ethical values and the loss of his previously sound judgment. He tends to become increasingly unreliable, lazy and often careless with the truth. Sometimes such people make a complete change and stop drinking. But they can never be restored to the sharp intellectual persons that they once were. They must adjust their lives to the level to which they've fallen ... Alcohol destroys both mind and personality.

The liquor industry makes approximately twelve billion dollars worth of sales each year after spending a half-billion dollars in advertising to bring more people under the addiction of strong drink. Something like six million alcoholics and another six million problem drinkers are already the victims of this conspiracy. It all begins with the beautiful, multi-colored pictures in the magazines, but it ends in that sordid, disturbing kind of scene that we preachers, counselors, law-enforcement officers, and doctors see.

What is the case for alcohol? There is no case. Alcohol destroys internally, externally, eternally. But what's the answer to the problem of alcohol? To the man who is not yet involved, it's "Leave it alone. Don't touch it. It's too dangerous to be touched, too dangerous to be tried." But what can be done for the man who is already hooked and even more especially for his tragically suffering family?

The Only Answer

What is the answer to the problem of drinking? What can we say to the person who has become involved? Some time ago I sat across the desk from a man whose life was being destroyed by alcohol. He poured out his heart to me. He told of his family and the relations that had deteriorated. He told of his business and of one job after another. After he finished I said, "But first of all, you need to be a Christian." And then I told him, "Your life is like a great locomotive that has been derailed. You need to be lifted back onto the track of purity and righteousness and start your life again."

He had been living for twenty-two years without ever having gone to church, and in those years he had lived his life in rebellion against many of the basic laws that God has given to guide men to happy and useful lives. I did not begin by telling him to quit drinking. He could not have done it; but after he became a Christian, after he had strengthened up the internal affairs of his life, after he was worshiping God, and after he was receiving the strength that Christ can give; then he found the power to overcome his problem. The apostle Paul said under very different circumstances and, yet, with universal application, "I can do all things in him that strengtheneth me" (Phil. 4:13).

Alcoholism usually comes upon those who have practiced social drinking and to whom alcohol is easily available. It usually comes when he feels some serious internal problem. The four great negative, destructive emotions that plague mankind are hatred and jealousy of others, fear of one kind or another, guilt from wrong-doing, and feelings of frustration and failure. When a person is feeling any one of these emotions, he is sorely tempted to escape by way of alcohol or by some other means. In addition, each human being has a great need to love someone and to be loved; otherwise he feels unfulfilled and devastatingly lonely. Each person also needs to be working and striving for goals that are important to him. When either love or goals are absent, one is tempted to escape by means of alcohol or something else. Obviously, proper counsel for such a person is not merely to stop drinking, but to fulfill the deep needs of his life and thereby remedy the causes of the alcohol problem. Here is where Christ comes in. He alone can supply the permanently satisfying goals that a well-balanced life must have. He alone can make a person the kind of man or woman who loves others and who is loved in return. Christ alone has the answer to the great destructive emotions of resentment, fear, guilt, and failure.

A New Man

To those who find themselves in a slough of despondency, we say, "Take hope; there is a place of beginning anew." No man can live his life over again; that is an utter impossibility. It is possible, however, through our Lord Jesus Christ, to begin anew. The apostle Paul wrote, ". . . if any man is in Christ, he is a new creature: the old things are passed away; behold, they are become new" (II Cor. 5:17). In another place we find him saying, ". . . put away, as concerning your former manner of life, the old man, that waxeth corrupt after the lusts of deceit; and that ye be renewed in the spirit of your mind, and put on the new man, that after God hath been created in righteousness and holiness of truth" (Eph. 4:22-24). Man's last but best hope is Christ. To begin anew, one must be in Christ. Jesus himself said, ". . . Ye must be born anew" (John 3:7). To be born anew we must come to Christ in faith. Paul puts it this way:

"For ye are all sons of God, through faith, in Christ Jesus." Then he adds, "For as many of you as were baptized into Christ did put on Christ" (Gal. 3:26, 27). To be in Christ is to start life anew.

If alcoholism is your problem, you, too, need to come to Christ and begin again. Sometimes a man who has sunk to the depths through the use of liquor says, "Oh, I can't come back. I've gone too far!" But this is not true. In I John 1:9 we read, "If we confess our sins, he is faithful and righteous to forgive us our sins, and to cleanse us from all unrighteousness."

Christ cleanses you and gives you the new life that you seek, making you a child of God and surrounding you with Christian friends who care and are concerned for your welfare. Don't underestimate the great strength that comes from being a child of God and don't underestimate the power of this warm Christian fellowship, of loving hearts that care. The Lord promises you that, as you let Him guide you, His strength and His power will be with you.

Do you remember the words of the apostle Paul in I Corinthians 10:13? "There hath no temptation taken you but such as man can bear: but God is faithful, who will not suffer you to be tempted above that ye are able; but will with the temptation make also the way of escape, that ye may be able to endure it." Then there are Paul's words in Colossians 1:27: ". . . Christ in you, the hope of glory." Finally, there are the words which our Lord spoke before leaving the earth, ". . . lo, I am with you always . . ." (Matt. 28:20). This is the answer to the alcohol problem.

8

The Golden Years

What can be said of a time characterized by physical weakness, forgetfulness, enforced idleness, impaired hearing and sight, and, above all, the loss of purpose and direction? Actually, a great deal can be said. Contrary to almost universal thinking, old age need not be dreaded; it may be a time of fulfillment.

However, one's later years will be golden only if, in one's earlier years, one was dedicated and shouldered responsibility. Happiness and fulfillment in old age do not come by accident. As the body ages, the mind must be rekindled from day to day. This takes some doing, but it can be done. A French philosopher once said: "The golden age is *before* us, not behind us."

Along with those of you who are rapidly approaching—or who may already have reached—the "Golden Years," I'm concerned about the problems, the frustrations, the needless heartaches that beset the aged. Even Moses was not immune to self-pity when he wrote: "The days of our years are threescore years and ten, Or even by reason of strength fourscore years; Yet is their pride but labor and sorrow; For it is soon gone, and we fly away" (Ps. 90:10). With this feeling of helplessness and hopelessness, man ends his days as he began them, by retreating to that world within, that place of isolation from both hurt and help.

But some men never seem to grow old. William Shakespeare described them as "always active in thought, always ready to adopt new ideas . . . never chargeable with fogyism. Satisfied, yet ever dissatisfied . . . settled, yet ever unsettled . . . they always enjoy the best of what is, and are the first to find the best of what will be."

"The best of what will be." What makes the difference? Why are some people so positive while others are so negative? The former have discovered a valued secret, that "age does not depend upon years, but upon temperament." With a renewing of the mind, there must also be a renewal of the spirit. "Renew a right spirit within me" (Ps. 51:10), David pleaded. And of this great man, burdened with problems and persecutions that would have crushed those around him, it was said that he "died in a good old age, full of days, riches and honor" (I Chron. 29:28).

Radiant Christian Lives

When I think of radiant Christian lives, I often think of Mrs. A. R. Holton. She and her husband devoted their long lives to serving others—he as a minister of the gospel of Christ and she as his worthy helpmeet and companion. They also reared three fine children. At the age of seventy, when most people are retired, they went as missionaries to Korea, taking with them maturity and experience that young people cannot. When her beloved husband died, Mrs. Holton showed a Christian maturity that is rare indeed. Neighbors and friends hurried in to express sympathy, but she showed no emotional upset, saying, "Don't worry about Daddy. This was the finest day of his life, the day for which he has been preparing all these years." Truly, it was a day of triumph. Lives like these are beautiful indeed.

I also think of my aged aunt, Mrs. Mae Legate. At eighty-three she amazed us by teaching her class of preschool children each Sunday. She not only taught them, she told them Bible stories in such a way that she delighted them. During the week she found time and energy to babysit for parents who, for one reason or another, needed to be away from home. She always had a twinkle in her eye and some interesting plan of activity underway. She had a heart condition, and had had major surgery for cancer, but she still outdistanced most of us. When we talked occasionally about her age and about growing old, she liked to say, "I'm still looking for a little bit of sugar in the bottom of the cup." We who knew her and loved her are sure that she found it.

The Glories of Age

The test of a people, a nation, or a culture, some have suggested, is how the aged are treated. It's easy to love little children, or to admire industrious youth. It is almost equally easy to ignore older people. Consequently, we are apt to live in fear of growing old. One sign of this is the amount of time, money, and energy we spend on the art of concealing the evidence of old age.

The Bible, in contrast to this, points to the glories of old age. In Proverbs, for example, it says that "a hoary head"—that is, an old and gray-haired head—"is a crown of glory; it is gained in a righteous life" (16:31 RSV), that "the glory of young men is their strength, but the beauty of old men is their gray hair" (20:29 RSV), and that those who keep God's commandments will be given "length of days and years of life and abundant welfare" (3:2 RSV). Age is not something to avoid, even if that were possible, but a time of mellowing and ripening which is to be anticipated.

When the apostle Paul faced the end of his life, he expressed the Christian viewpoint quite eloquently: "I have fought the good fight, I have finished the race, I have kept the faith. Henceforth there is laid up for me the crown of righteousness, which the Lord, the righteous judge, will award to me on that Day, and not only to me but also to all who have loved his appearing" (II Tim. 4:7, 8 RSV).

Special Needs

Are there ways to prevent the isolation, loneliness, and depression of old age that so often seem to be inseparable from it?

Perhaps a beginning can be made by thinking about the special needs of older people. One is *a sense of usefulness*. The happiest older people appear to be those who have found a renewed usefulness after their retirement from lifelong careers.

A retired businessman may lend his wisdom to operators of small businesses or firms in underdeveloped areas. A retired teacher may help retarded or deprived children grow in self-confidence and capability. Reading to the blind, visiting the ill, training the young, or using one's own abilities in handicrafts which tend to be forgotten in our machine-driven age are just a few ways in which older people have found fulfillment.

But we need to remind ourselves that the worth of a person is not determined by his physical usefulness to society. No one wants to be appreciated merely because of what he is worth to others. The glory of the stars or of a redwood tree is not limited to the functions these fulfill, nor is the glory of a human life, created in the image of God. We do need activities which are suited to our abilities, but when physical and mental activities are curtailed or ended by our health, we are still valuable simply because we are human beings.

A second need which older persons sense is *personal fulfillment*. They need recreation and entertainment. If older people stagnate spiritually, they become bored and empty. Only if we could enter older age the way we entered our senior year of high school and of college, with excitement and hope for the future, life would take on a new quality.

Karle Wilson Baker has expressed this desire for fulfillment in older age in a beautiful poem:

> Let me grow lovely, growing old—
>   So many fine things do;
> Laces, and ivory, and gold,
>   And silks need not be new;
> And there is healing in old trees,
>   Old streets a glamour hold;
> Why may not I, as well as these,
>   Grow lovely, growing old?

The Bible recognizes the maturity and wisdom which can

come only with age, reserving certain tasks for older people to perform. Leadership in the church during the New Testament period was provided by men who were chosen from within the congregation, whose lives had certain qualities. These men are called bishops or overseers in some Scripture passages because of their work as guardians or superintendents of the church (I Tim. 3:1, 2; Acts 20:28). In other passages they are designated pastors or shepherds, an analogy between their guidance of Christians and the shepherd's caring for his sheep (Eph. 4:11; 1 Peter 5:1-4). The older person who exercises leadership in the church and who has prepared himself for it cannot help but feel useful and very fulfilled.

The apostle Paul indicated to Titus that older men and women are to be teachers and examples to younger persons (2:1-5). If this teaching were taken more seriously today, it would have a tremendous effect upon our home life!

The aging person not only needs to feel that he is useful and that life is still full of meaning, he also needs *security*. Loneliness, illness, or even the fear of passing time may result in a serious loss of self-confidence. One of our defenses against such emotional problems is to allow them to be carried over into bodily pains.

The family may not be concerned about the emotional pain of an older person, but physical pain may create family anxiety and reassure the older person that he is still important.

The exact source of our pain is often difficult for us to know, but a great deal of suffering at any age is traceable to our longing for security—the security we gain only through the knowledge that other people care. Even our reflections on the "good old days" may be exaggerated by the loneliness and pain of the present moment.

To recall our past accomplishments is to reassure ourselves of our personal worth. And yet, the older person needs a dream for the future, not just a memory of the past.

Problems To Be Faced

But how about those who have given up? What about that loved one of yours? Or you, yourself? Jonathan Swift expressed the feelings of many when he said, "Everyone desires to live long, but no one would be old."

Loneliness is a common complaint, experienced on occasion by the young but usually reserved for the aged. Added to loneliness in old age is the spectre of disillusionment—disillusionment with government, morality, and friends and dear ones, who so often give cause for disillusionment.

And there is worry. Someone has observed that "worry is interest paid on trouble before it becomes due." At the conclusion of His great message concerning the place of material things in a man's life, Jesus said, "Be not therefore anxious for the morrow: for the morrow will be anxious for itself. Sufficient unto the day is the evil thereof" (Matt. 6:34).

So, instead of golden years, these last precious moments are years of bitterness and self-pity. In place of a golden sunset are dark clouds of discontent and chilly winds of sorrow.

If old age had to be this way, what a drab prospect it would present to us all. But your life and my life need not be gloomy and sad. The power of the human spirit is capable, with God's help, of rising above the transient heartaches, conquering the demons of doubt, and holding fast to a saving faith in God's goodness and in His power to save.

Pitfalls in the Way

Some time ago, a national weekly carried a feature article on the pitfalls in the path of older people. Entitled "Charlie's Morbid Fears," it stated that Charlie, who was—as the cliche has it—getting along in years, knew that "the golden years" were a myth. Charlie, it seems, had seen what happened to older members of his own family, his wife's family, and friends' families. He saw "the shadowy landscape beyond age 65 concealing a ghastly minefield: heart disease to the left of him, malignant growths to the right of him, and you-name-it up ahead." Worse still, Charlie had nightmares of staring blankly at a television set with other oldtimers in the seedy common room of the Sunset Years Nursing Home.

The article specified some of the foolish popular misconceptions about old age: the average person over sixty-five is isolated, lonely, extremely unhappy, and beset with various diseases and calamities. It's true that life is not easy for many elderly people, but is it easy for anyone? The elderly are quite capable of being resourceful, optimistic, and cheerful. The stereotype of a complaining, dissatisfied, and spiritually displaced person is unfair to the majority of the twenty million Americans who are over sixty-five. Only four percent are confined to nursing homes and a scant one percent are in mental hospitals. A recent national poll indicates that a vast majority of the nation's old people are satisfied with retirement.

Most young people consider old age a time when men and women become irritable with infirmities and lost in yesterday's world. This need not be so. One authority, Peter Chew, states that "old age should be a great adventure of the spirit." Ray Palmer, a nineteenth-century preacher and poet, wrote, "Instead of [old age] bringing sad and melancholy prospects of decay, it should give us hopes of eternal youth in a better world." The trick is to grow old with dignity, intelligence, and flair.

Even illness can serve a purpose. I recall the experience of a friend who, while recovering from a serious illness, was advised by his doctor to take a long walk every day. In the course of following the doctor's instructions, my friend realized that he had forgotten how beautiful white clouds in the blue sky can be. He began to see beauty and majesty even in storm clouds, to hear the singing of birds, and to see various forms of life in fields and streams. Even when he went to the city, despite all of the pollution and crime, he was able, because of his serenity, to be at peace and to notice otherwise unnoticed acts of kindness and consideration. He learned slowly that giving is the first order of getting, or, as Jesus put it, ". . . whatsoever ye would that men should do unto you, even so do ye also unto them" (Matt. 7:12).

Only recently, psychologists have been urging the elderly to learn how to accept with serenity their station in life and reflect on the purpose of life.

A Most Meaningful Prayer

"God grant me the serenity to accept the things I cannot

change, courage to change the things I can and wisdom to know the difference." Those twenty-seven words may well be the best-loved and most widely known prayer written in the twentieth century. Millions of copies of this prayer were distributed by the U.S.O. during World War II. Alcoholics Anonymous adopted it as an official motto, and you may well have a copy of the words somewhere in your home—perhaps on a wooden plaque, in a mounted inscription, or on a bookmark in the family Bible.

The author of the prayer seems to have attached no unusual significance to it; he appears to have prepared it for a Sunday worship service without thought of using it again. But its message has struck thousands of people. Serenity to accept what we cannot change . . . courage to change what we can change . . . and wisdom to discern between what we can and cannot change. This is the quality of life that we all want.

We all live with these two kinds of circumstances. Some realities we cannot change with any amount of effort. We have to adapt ourselves to them because they will not adapt themselves to us. Perhaps we must live with a handicap, or a great personal loss, or a terrifying fear, or an awesome responsibility; the only approach we can take to such hostile circumstances is one of calm courage. Some realities—persons, things, circumstances— we can change with effort. We are in daily need of wisdom to distinguish between these two types of realities and to face them squarely.

How Does One Cope?

But how do I plan for old age? It is easy enough to analyze special problems and needs of aging people, but how do I cope with them? Preparation for older age is a lifelong process. We prepare ourselves for retirement during the days of our youth, whether we realize it or not. We make provision for a financial income during old age; how can we ensure a spiritual income for old age? I have gleaned several suggestions from older persons, and those trained to understand and work with older people, and I am convinced that they are useful for both older persons and younger people interested in preparing for retirement.

The first suggestion is to *consider life a "sowing and reaping"* process. To rear one's family well, to do so much good for others that their gratitude can never be exhausted, to work hard enough in life so that one can look back upon duties well done: these are among the surest guarantees of a happy old age.

An inner purification is even more important than the development of hobbies and recreation which one will enjoy in older age. A worthy goal is to work, with God's gracious help, toward the elimination of resentment, bitterness, quarreling, jealousy, and fault-finding.

A second hint is to *prepare for older age by developing a proper attitude toward service.* Many public service projects need older persons. However, one should not think of work as a necessity during retirement; poor health or other reasons, might prevent it. The important thing is for people of every age group to engage in truly human activities. Work is only one such activity; there are many others that serve one's fellowman.

Third, *retain your self-respect during your older years.* This involves proper personal care, tidiness about dress, planning your diet, and not apologizing for one's age. Young people seldom apologize for their lack of experience—something they cannot help; older people need not apologize for limitations which they cannot help.

Also, *listen to other people rather than giving them advice which they may not want.* If one can learn to endure his aches and pains with a minimum of complaint and to reserve his advice until it is sought, he may find himself considered an asset rather than a liability. People may even begin to consult him as a kind of travel guide who knows the best roads to follow through life.

Accept physical and mental limitations gracefully. This may involve voluntarily surrendering your driver's license, or just keeping out of the way of active younger people whose own burdens may be heavier than you realize.

Communicate with other people. If your companion is living and you are able to talk frankly about mutual problems and possibilities, and if you are able to keep in touch with old friends while making reasonable efforts to make new friends, your life will be enriched. On the other hand, maintain whatever independence you can. This does not mean you should be reluctant to accept help from others, but that you should not allow yourself to be pampered and coddled, something which is inimical to the strong spirit of which you are capable. Twenty million men and women in the United States are older than sixty-five, and their votes, influence, and spending power should afford them a measure of independence. And as that number increases, the walls that segregate older from younger should break down more easily as each of us bears his own responsibilities as fully as possible.

Place high value on time. If one thinks only of ways to "pass the day away," he fails to achieve many things that are within his reach: an hour with a book that will give new insights or a new strength of spirit; an hour with music or poetry that will do the same; an hour of visiting someone who is lonely; an hour in a hospital comforting someone; an hour in a worship service or in private study of the Word of God; an hour with one's lifelong companion, recalling the joys of earlier years that assure you, "the best is yet to be."

Time is valuable for all of us, but it is most valuable to the older person, who should prize every hour.

Cultivate a sense of humor that will allow you to enjoy laughing with others. This is the best antidote to the tendency of taking yourself too seriously and of turning your eyes inward and seeing only sadness.

The climax of these suggestions for growing older gracefully is, *grow spiritually.* Read at least a few verses of the Bible daily and reflect on them quietly. Keep your prayers uncomplicated but make them frequent. Carl Jung, the late Swiss psychoanalyst, wrote this interesting observation about his patients "in the second half of life—that is to say, over thirty-five." He said that "there has not been one whose problem in the last resort was not of finding a religious outlook on life. It is safe to say that every one of them fell ill because he had lost that which the living religions of every age have given to their followers, and none of them has been really healed who did not regain his religious outlook." The development of spiritual resources is

important during every period of one's life and provides deep
wells of strength for the older years.

The Spiritual Dimension

Evelyn Underhill wrote a treatise on the human soul in which
she said, "The soul lives in a two-story house. The upper floor is
the supernatural, spiritual life with a capacity for God." The
tragedy of life is spending all of one's days, including old age, on
the lower level. "For what good is it for a man to gain the whole
world," asks Jesus, "at the price of his own soul?" (Matt. 16:26
Phillips).

Many years ago, English author G. K. Chesterton submitted
a motto for the Chicago Exposition: "The world will never starve
for wonders, but only for want of wonder." When a man or
woman takes a sense of wonder into the ripe years of maturity,
he or she is at peace and contented. When he wonders at the
magnitude of God's love, he will, as a natural consequence, fully
accept God's will. Lelia Morris expressed it in this manner:

> My stubborn will at last hath yielded;
> I would be Thine and Thine alone;
> And this the prayer my lips are bringing,
> "Lord, let in me Thy will be done."
> Thy precious will, O conqu'ring Savior,
> Doth now embrace and compass me;
> All discords hushed, my peace a river,
> My soul a prisoned bird set free.

Someone has said, "An aged Christian, with the snow of time
upon his head, may remind us that those points of earth are
whitest which are nearest to heaven." Another author his written,
"The older a man grows the more mysterious life becomes to
him. We sometimes say to a youth that when he grows up he will
know more, but that is a half-truth. In general, an increasing
experience of life only deepens the sense of its mystery." One
retains his sense of wonder when he grows in the grace and
knowledge of our Lord and Savior Jesus Christ (II Peter 3:18).

Work To Be Done

We see a case in point in Enoch Pound as he neared his nine-
tieth year. In the preface to his highly informative book, *Con-
versations on the Bible,* Dr. Pound said:

> This work is the child of my old age. My reasons for preparing
> it have been partly personal. I needed something to do. I must
> have some steady congenial employment, or I could not be happy.
> I felt, too, that if I neglected to employ my faculties, I might
> soon lose them. The best mode of preserving them unimpaired
> would be to keep them bright with use. At the same time, I could
> think of nothing on which, at my period of life, I could more
> appropriately employ my thoughts than on the Bible. I firmly
> believe it to be a revelation from God to the world—a "light
> shining in a dark place;" I had made it, in one form or another,
> the study of a long life; my sentiments in regard to it were
> matured and settled; and what better could I do than to pass
> over its sacred contents in the form of question and answer, and
> set them forth for the instruction and benefit of my fellow men?

It is good for the aged to realize that they are not beyond the
instruction of God's holy Word. The Bible has much to tell us
about growing old.

In his Letter to Titus, the apostle Paul advises "that aged men
be temperate, grave, sober-minded, sound in faith, in love, in
patience: that aged women likewise be reverent in demeanor,
not slanderers nor enslaved to much wine, teachers of that which
is good; that they may train the young women to love their
husbands, to love their children, to be sober-minded, chaste,
workers at home, kind, being in subjection to their own
husbands, that the word of God be not blasphemed" (2:2-5).
The psalmist said of the righteous, "They shall still bring forth
fruit in old age" (92:14).

An interesting sidelight relating to old age is recorded in the
opening pages of Genesis. "And all the days of Methuselah were
nine hundred sixty and nine years: and he died" (5:27). The
Bible mentions nothing about worthwhile qualities of Methuselah
except that he lived longer than any other man. The years were
many, but were they golden? He had length, but what of
breadth and depth and height? In one of the great passages of

the New Testament, Paul prays "that Christ may dwell in your hearts through faith; to the end that ye, being rooted and grounded in love, may be strong to apprehend with all the saints what is the breadth and length and height and depth, and to know the love of Christ which passeth knowledge, that ye may be filled unto all the fulness of God" (Eph. 3:17-19).

A passage that offers a great challenge to anyone who feels "over the hill," is addressed by Paul to the Philippians: "Not that I have already obtained, or am already made perfect: but I press on, if so be that I may lay hold on that for which also I was laid hold on by Christ Jesus. Brethren, I count not myself yet to have laid hold: but one thing I do, forgetting the things which are behind, and stretching forward to the things which are before, I press on toward the goal unto the prize of the high calling of God in Christ Jesus." A few lines later he reminds us that "our citizenship is in heaven" (3:12-14, 20).

"Old age is a blessed time. It gives us leisure to put off our earthly garments one by one, and dress ourselves for heaven. 'Blessed are they that are homesick, for they shall get home.'" Jesus knew what this meant. And although He was only thirty-three when He died on the cross, He knew the feeling of loneliness. He was alone when He prayed by Himself in the Garden of Gethsemane, "My Father, if it be possible, let this cup pass away from me" (Matt. 26:39). All of us, sooner or later, find ourselves in our own personal Gethsemane. May we say with Him, "not my will, but thine, be done" (Luke 22:42).

Looking Forward

In so many ways the Bible indicates to us both that life gets *better* as it progresses and that life gets *harder*. Most of us have a strong tendency toward nostalgia; we are afraid of the unknown future and we tend to fantasize the "good old days." The Israelites, during the exodus and the wilderness wanderings, did this. Life was difficult for them, so they recalled the onions and garlic which they had in Egypt. They preferred a return to slavery in Egypt to pressing forward toward Canaan (Num. 11:4-6). People who observed Jesus decided He must be some great prophet of the past who had returned to earth—perhaps

John the Baptist, Elijah, Jeremiah, or one of the other prophets;
they couldn't imagine that one of their contemporaries could be
as great a leader as those of the past (Matt. 16:13, 14). When
left to our own thoughts, particularly as we grow older, we are
tempted to glorify the past and to dread the future.

And yet, the religion of the Bible is basically a religion of
promise, not of nostalgia. Its direction from the earliest times
was forward, not backward. When God called Abraham, He
pointed him toward the future: "Go from your country and your
kindred and your father's house to the land that I will show
you. And I will make of you a great nation, and I will bless you,
and make your name great, so that you will be a blessing"
(Gen. 12:1, 2 RSV).

When He called Moses, God challenged him with promises
for the future: "Come, I will send you to Pharoah that you may
bring forth my people, the sons of Israel, out of Egypt" (Exod.
3:10 RSV). God was and is a God of *promise;* with our lives in
His hands, "the best is yet to be."

Never Alone

Jesus was alone when Peter and all the other apostles forsook
Him. He was alone when He stood before Pilate and admitted
He was a King. He was alone, though jeering unbelievers
jostled Him, as He staggered under the weight of His cross. He
was alone when He cried, "My God, my God, why hast thou
forsaken me" (Mark 15:34). Jesus was alone, and, yet, He was
never alone. And here is the key that opens the door to security,
to hope, to happiness, to a full share of peace and contentment.

Jesus said, "Behold, the hour cometh, yea, is come, that ye
shall . . . leave me alone: and yet I am not alone, because the
Father is with me" (John 16:32).

Frederick Robertson, a man who received a full share of hard
blows during his short life, had this to say: "Do not go timor-
ously about enquiring what others say. Believe in God. God is
near you. Throw yourself fearlessly upon Him. Trembling mortal,
there is an unknown might within your soul which will wake
when you command it. The day may come when all that is
human—man and woman—will fall off from you, as they did

from Him. Let His strength be yours. Be independent of them all now. The Father is with you. Look to Him, and He will save you." In Browning's perceptive poem, "Rabbi Ben Ezra," are the lines:

> Grow old along with me!
> The best is yet to be,
> The last of life, for which
>   the first was made:
> Our times are in his hand
> Who saith, "A whole I planned,
> Youth shows but half; trust God:
>   see all, nor be afraid!"

As Moses approached the end of his life, he blessed each of the tribes of Israel. Moses had been so concerned about Israel's ingratitude—her sinfulness and apostasy—but he concluded his final instructions with a note of hope.

Moses' blessing on the tribe of Asher was: "And as thy days, so shall thy strength be" (Deut. 33:25). May you have strength sufficient to face what life brings; isn't that what all of us want and need? This will give us serenity in the face of circumstances we cannot change and courage to deal with those we can.

Moses then pronounced a final blessing on the whole nation of Israel: "There is none like God . . . who rides through the heavens to your help, and in his majesty through the skies. The eternal God is your dwelling place, and underneath are the everlasting arms" (Deut. 33:26, 27 RSV).

9

The Burden
of Grief

"Every man can master a grief but he that has it," says Benedict in Shakespeare's *Much Ado About Nothing,* and this is too close to the truth for comfort. Grief is gnawing, throbbing, insistent. It clings tenaciously. Even in moments of elation, dismal thoughts often creep into our consciousness and, in too many instances, grief-laden thoughts determine our outlook and disposition.

We are all familiar with the word *grief.* Most of us are acquainted not only with the word but also with the experience. It is a common word and an experience common to most of us. The dictionary defines *grief* as "mental suffering from bereavement, remorse, or the like." Sooner or later all of us will know the meaning of grief in a very personal way.

There is much physical pain and suffering in our world. Think of the pain involved in childbirth, broken bones, severe cuts, bad burns, and gunshot wounds. These, in a sense, are external, physical pains. There is also pain and suffering of the mind, and this is what we call grief or sorrow.

On one occasion the apostle Paul spoke of his many persecutions: "Of the Jews five times received I forty stripes save one.

Thrice was I beaten with rods, once was I stoned, thrice I suffered shipwreck, a night and a day have I been in the deep." Then in contrast he said, "Besides those things that are without, there is that which presseth upon me daily, anxiety for all the churches" (II Cor. 11:24, 28). His "anxieties" were caused by the divisions in some churches and the apostasy of some disciples. In II Timothy 4:10 he grieved over one of these disciples: "Demas hath forsaken me, having loved this present world" (AV). These sorrows and griefs are within the mind and heart.

External and internal suffering are closely related: man's physical problems are a constant burden on the human spirit. The body is destined for decline and ultimate decay. Disease, accidents, hunger, disappointment, frustration, guilt, and disillusionment are a few of the miseries that grieve the heart. Men grieve over lost causes, lost opportunities, broken friendships, broken homes, and, of course, death.

Grief Is Universal

Nothing is more true than that grief is universal. For example, the first man and woman on earth, Adam and Eve, knew the pangs of grief—when they discovered the lifeless body of their son Abel, and when they realized he had been murdered by their oldest son Cain. In the months and years that followed, with Cain estranged from the rest of the family and banished to another part of the earth, their grief must have been heavy. Especially so when they also remembered their own earlier disobedience to God. Perhaps they even felt the anguish that comes from parents' realization that their sins made possible their children's sins.

We could choose from characters in the Bible almost at random for another example of a person who knew the inner hurt of grief, but let us look at David. In Psalm 38:17 he wrote, "My sorrow is continually before me." In Psalm 51:1-3, he added, "Have mercy upon me, O God, according to thy lovingkindness: according to the multitude of thy tender mercies blot out my transgressions. Wash me thoroughly from mine iniquity, and cleanse me from my sin. For I know my transgressions; and my sin is ever before me." Night and day, wherever he went, for as long as he lived, his sin flashed periodically before his eyes.

In the latter part of his life David experienced still another form of grief. His son Absalom, the apple of his eye, led a rebellion against him that forced David to flee Jerusalem and seek safety in the wilderness. Eventually, however, David's army discovered Absalom and, in disobedience to David's command, slew Absalom. After a messenger told David of his son's death, he said, "O my son Absalom, my son, my son Absalom! would I had died for thee, O Absalom, my son, my son!" (II Sam. 18:33). David loved Absalom too much to rejoice in his death, even though it meant the end of the rebellion. David grieved greatly.

Another Old Testament example is Job. He lost his seven sons and three daughters, as well as his vast possessions, which included seven thousand sheep, three thousand camels, oxen, and other livestock. To this was added the physical discomfort of boils. All of this happened during just a few short days and he who had been blessed so greatly was brought down to the depths of despair. Three friends came to console him, but the Scripture says that "they sat down with him upon the ground seven days and seven nights, and none spake a word unto him: for they saw that his grief was very great" (2:13). It is well for us to remember that Job retained his integrity, God ended his trials, and God blessed him.

The Lord, Also

More impressive even than the grief experienced by these men of old was that experienced by our Lord. Seven centuries before Christ's birth Isaiah prophesied that "He was despised, and rejected of men; a man of sorrows, and acquainted with grief . . . Surely he hath borne our griefs, and carried our sorrows . . . Yet it pleased Jehovah to bruise him; he hath put him to grief . . ." (53:3, 4, 10). In Matthew 23:37, 38 we see one major cause for His grief, the rejection of His salvation by the people of His own time. Looking over the city of Jerusalem, he said, "O Jerusalem, Jerusalem, that killeth the prophets, and stoneth them that are sent unto her! how often would I have gathered thy children together, even as a hen gathereth her chickens under her wings, and ye would not! Behold, your house is left unto you desolate."

On the night of his betrayal in the garden of Gethsemane, Jesus also felt deep grief: "And he came out, and went, as his custom was, unto the mount of Olives; and the disciples also followed him . . . And he was parted from them about a stone's cast; and he kneeled down and prayed, saying, Father, if thou be willing, remove this cup from me: nevertheless not my will, but thine, be done . . . And being in an agony he prayed more earnestly; and his sweat became as it were great drops of blood falling down upon the ground" (Luke 22:39, 41-44).

Nor did the Son alone know the agony of grief; even the Father himself has suffered this anguish. Some generations after the creation of Adam and Eve, "Jehovah saw that the wickedness of man was great in the earth, and that every imagination of the thoughts of his heart was only evil continually. And it repented Jehovah that he had made man on the earth, and it grieved him at his heart" (Gen. 6:5, 6). The grief experienced by the men and women reported in the Bible came to an end, but that which our Lord and our God felt so long ago when men turned away in rebellion continues until this hour and will continue until the end of time. God is still grieved by man's willful rejection of His better way of life.

When we, individually, have to face grief, it is some help to know that all men who have lived before us, as well as all of our contemporaries, also have known grief. Of even more help is the knowledge that the divine Son of God and even God Himself have not been above this especially painful kind of suffering. We are certainly not alone when we grieve.

Strength in Christ

We find strength to overcome our grief in Christ. The Bible approaches the problems of life and death quite realistically. There is no glossing over. Never are we promised freedom from the suffering and anguish which are so common in this world. Never are we deceived about what lies ahead on the earth. Disappointment, decay, and death are inevitable for all.

However, in Christ we do find the strength to overcome our

grief. He has given us hope for a better world. He has also given us higher goals for which to live. If our lives were centered in this world, inevitably life would be a tragedy. Christ has taught us to center our lives in the more wonderful world to come, the spiritual world.

Paul wrote to the Corinthians: "If we have only hoped in Christ in this life, we are of all men most pitiable. But now hath Christ been raised from the dead, the firstfruits of them that are asleep" (I Cor. 15:19, 20). To the Philippians he wrote, "I count all things to be loss for the excellency of the knowledge of Christ Jesus my Lord: for whom I suffered the loss of all things, and do count them but refuse, that I may gain Christ . . . For our citizenship is in heaven" (3:8, 20).

In a second letter to the Corinthians Paul wrote, "Wherefore we faint not; but though our outward man is decaying, yet our inward man is renewed day by day. For our light affliction, which is for the moment, worketh for us more and more exceedingly an eternal weight of glory; while we look not at the things which are seen, but at the things which are not seen: for the things which are seen are temporal; but the things which are not seen are eternal" (4:16-18). To the Thessalonians he wrote, "But we would not have you ignorant, brethren, concerning them that fall asleep; that ye sorrow not, even as the rest, who have no hope. For if we believe that Jesus died and rose again, even so them also that are fallen asleep in Jesus will God bring with him" (I Thess. 4:13, 14). Finally, from the apostle John we have these encouraging words concerning the life that is to come. God "shall wipe away every tear from their eyes; and death shall be no more, neither shall there be mourning, nor crying, nor pain, any more: the first things are passed away" (Rev. 21:4).

Griefs Can Be Blessings

Our heartaches and trials in this life often prove to be blessings. James says to "count it all joy, my brethren, when ye fall into manifold temptations [RSV: trials]; knowing that the proving of your faith worketh patience" (1:2, 3). In the Roman letter we read, "We also rejoice in our tribulations: knowing that tribulation worketh stedfastness; and stedfastness, approvedness; and approvedness, hope; and hope putteth not to shame; because the love of God hath been shed abroad in our hearts through the Holy Spirit which was given unto us" (5:3-5).

Harry Emerson Fosdick once said that "adversity, far from being a nuisance or cruelty, is one of the constituent elements of great living, to be finely used. When you and I have a personal calamity and have handled it well, we have always added a new dimension to our character . . . When real adversity comes, a soul true to itself builds new dimensions. And some people who have lived like that, simply by being what they are, have helped us more than all the busy folk who serve us with their hands—they triumphed in their troubles."

Through our griefs and sorrows we often come to a brighter, better world. As the Strait of Gibraltar seems to close like a gate behind the ship that has passed through it from the Mediterranean, so death and other of life's crises seem to close us in from life. However, as the broad expanses of the Atlantic open wide beyond the Strait, so do the beautiful vistas of eternity open wide to the Christian beyond death. Christ is our Pilot on a voyage that is often dark and stormy from earth to heaven.

Suggestions

Dr. M. Norvel Young, chancellor of Pepperdine University in Los Angeles and a long-time friend, has suggested six ways to overcome grief:

> 1) *Accept the sympathy of others graciously.* Sometimes they will not know how to express themselves well, but their love is sincere and you help them and yourself in leaning on them for a time.
>
> 2) *Recognize that the pain will grow more bearable.* The pain of sorrow is acute, but time will help, or rather we should say God will help and he uses time to heal our hurts.
>
> 3) *Turn to the Bible with renewed thirst.* Someone has said, "I opened the old, old Bible, and looked at a page of Psalms 'til the wintry sea of my troubles was soothed as by summer calms; for the words that have helped so many, and the ages have made more clear, seemed new in their power to comfort, as they brought me their word of cheer."

4) *Utilize the power of prayer.* As Tennyson said, "There is more wrought by prayer than this world dreams of." In the words of Frank L. Cox, "Divine comfort is greatly needed. Hearts are broken, bowed down with sorrow, filled with fear. Anxiety, bereavement, and temptation beset us. A humble prayer to "the God of all comfort" brings relief, binds up the broken heart, lightens the burden. Through prayer Jesus found relief and obtained strength to face the foe."

5) *Be even more faithful in worship.* Some people make the mistake of withdrawing from the world and of closing the blinds and locking the door. The wise Christian knows that worshipping with others who have suffered will help him. He knows that grief is a common denominator and that the solace of worship will be especially helpful at this time.

6) *Look out and see others who need your help.* Work is a blessing when we need to overcome sorrow. There is no substitute for getting busy helping others. The best way to honor the dead is to serve the living.

Many years ago John Keble, the English preacher-poet, wrote "Sun of My Soul." Peter Ritter set it to music, and it is now known and loved the world over. It strikes a responsive chord in all who have known grief and suffering.

> Sun of my soul, Thou Savior dear,
> It is not night if Thou be near;
> O may no earth-born cloud arise
> To hide Thee from Thy servant's eyes.

> When the soft dews of kindly sleep
> My wearied eye-lids gently steep,
> Be my last tho't, how sweet to rest
> For ever on my Savior's breast.

Perhaps you are familiar with Annie Johnson Flynt's poem:

> God hath not promised
> Sun without rain
> Joy without sorrow
> Peace without pain,
> But God hath promised
> Strength for the day,

Rest for the labor,
Light for the Way,
Grace for the trials
Help from above,
Unfailing sympathy
Undying love.

Paul's words give great encouragement: "I can do all things in him that strengtheneth me" (Phil. 4:13). "For I am persuaded, that neither death, nor life, nor angels, nor principalities, nor things present, nor things to come, nor powers, nor height, nor depth, nor any other creature, shall be able to separate us from the love of God, which is in Christ Jesus our Lord" (Rom. 8:38).

10

The Finality

of Death

Some time ago an elderly man, hospitalized by a serious illness, heard that an acquaintance had died. He thought for a long moment and then said simply, "Well, that's something we all must do." If death were the end of everything and only the blackness of nothingness lay ahead, life would be painfully bleak. But death, though inevitable, can be—in fact must be—an adventurous step into a glorious beyond. The apostle Paul wrote, "Death is swallowed up in victory" (I Cor. 15:54). His view of death was affirmative.

The Magnitude of Death

This planet has been referred to as a vast graveyard. With land becoming ever more precious, highrise mausoleums are being built and cremation is becoming commonplace. We have become so callous about funerals that many have no qualms about cutting in on a slow-moving cortege. However, when death singles out our own loved ones, our callousness melts away.

I have long been deeply impressed by these lines from John Donne's *Devotions:* "No man is an island, entire of itself; every man is a piece of the continent, a part of the main. If a clod be washed away by the sea, Europe is the less, as well as if a promontory were, as well as if a manor of thy friend's or of thine own were: any man's death diminishes me, because I am involved in mankind, and therefore never send to know for whom the bell tolls; it tolls for thee."

We find it difficult, before death strikes close to us, to comprehend the magnitude of death. In one of his famous sermons, "Victory Over Death," Frederick W. Robertson, the great Scottish preacher, said:

It is no mark of courage to speak lightly of human dying. We may do it in bravado, or in wantonness; but no man who thinks can call it a trifling thing to die. True thoughtfulness must shrink from death without Christ. There is a world of untold sensations prodded into that moment when a man [realizes] his hour is come. It is all over—his chance is passed, and his eternity is settled. None of us know, except by guess, what that sensation is. Myriads of human beings have felt it to whom life was dear; but they never spoke out their feelings, for such things are untold. And to every individual man throughout all eternity that sensation in its fullness can come but once. It is mockery . . . for a man to speak lightly about that which we cannot know till it comes.

Several years ago Russell V. DeLong enumerated four "Facts We Hate to Face": "Fact No. 1 . . . We are growing old. Fact No. 2 . . . We reap what we sow. Fact No. 3 . . . We must die. Fact No. 4 . . . There is a judgment." In summation he wrote: "We all hate to face these four disturbing facts. But we must face them. Therefore let us meet them honestly, so that we may: grow old happily . . . reap a good harvest because we have sown good seed . . . face death fearlessly because we trust Christ completely . . . stand at the judgment confidently because we have lived righteously."

Many a man has been able to joke about death—until death stares him in the face. Then death's inevitability and magnitude strike fear to his heart. The Bible tells us, "It is appointed unto men once to die, and after this cometh judgment" (Heb. 9:27). However, we need not face death fraught with fear. For the

Christian, the hour of death is one of triumph, as John Donne wrote in the poem, "Death Be Not Proud":

> Death be not proud, though some have called thee
> Mighty and dreadful, for, thou are not so,
> For, those, whom thou think'st, thou dost overthrow,
> Die not, poor death, nor yet canst thou kill me . . .
> One short sleep past, we wake eternally,
> And death shall be no more; death, thou shalt die.

Too many men have a negative attitude toward death, seeing only the fearful side. It is much wiser and fully justified to concentrate on the positive side. I like the words of Norman Macleod: "We picture death as coming to destroy; let us rather picture Christ as coming to save. We think of death as ending; let us rather think of life as beginning, and that more abundantly. We think of losing; let us think of gaining. We think of parting; let us think of meeting. We think of going away; let us think of arriving. And as the voice of death whispers 'You must go from earth,' let us hear the voice of Christ saying, 'You are but coming to me!' "

How the Scriptures Speak of Death

The world's keenest minds have often turned to the subject of death. The world's greatest writers have written much concerning death. Although men have written well and often concerning this subject, the God-inspired Scriptures are infinitely superior to any other writings on this most interesting theme. Some fifteen hundred years before the time of Christ, Moses wrote, "The days of our years are threescore years and ten, or even by reason of strength fourscore years; Yet is their pride but labor and sorrow; for it is soon gone, and we fly away" (Ps. 90:10). Much later, James asked the question, "What is your life?" He answered it simply but accurately, "For ye are a vapor that appeareth for a little time, and then vanisheth away" (4:14). The brevity of life and the inevitability of death are mentioned over and over in the Scriptures, as well they should be.

In speaking of His own approaching death, Jesus said to His

disciples, "The hour is come that the Son of man should be glorified. Verily, verily, I say unto you, Except a grain of wheat fall into the earth and die, it abideth by itself alone; but if it die, it beareth much fruit. He that loveth his life loseth it; and he that hateth his life in this world shall keep it unto life eternal" (John 12:23-25). Jesus also said, "Behold, we go up to Jerusalem; and the Son of man shall be delivered unto the chief priests and scribes; and they shall condemn him to death, and shall deliver him unto the Gentiles to mock, and to scourge, and to crucify: and the third day he shall be raised up" (Matt. 20:18-19). In numerous passages Jesus spoke of His resurrection.

The Scriptures speak just as explicitly of the resurrection of all men. They emphasize the resurrection of Christ's disciples, but also make it clear that all men will be raised. The apostle Paul wrote to the Thessalonians: "We would not have you ignorant, brethren, concerning them that fall asleep; that ye sorrow not, even as the rest, who have no hope. For if we believe that Jesus died and rose again, even so them also that are fallen asleep in Jesus will God bring with him" (I Thess. 4:13-14). In his first letter to the Corinthians, Paul said the most about the Christian's hope of resurrection: "If we have only hoped in Christ in this life, we are of all men most pitiable . . . So also is the resurrection of the dead. It is sown in corruption; it is raised in incorruption: it is sown in dishonor; it is raised in glory: it is sown in weakness; it is raised in power: it is sown a natural body; it is raised a spiritual body. If there is a natural body, there is also a spiritual body" (15:19, 42-44).

Later in the same chapter, Paul continued: "Now this I say, brethren, that flesh and blood cannot inherit the kingdom of God; neither doth corruption inherit incorruption. Behold, I tell you a mystery: We all shall not sleep, but we shall all be changed, in a moment, in the twinkling of an eye, at the last trump: for the trumpet shall sound, and the dead shall be raised incorruptible, and we shall be changed" (vv. 50-52). In view of this great fact, Paul could say: "For to me to live is Christ, and to die is gain . . . I am in a strait betwixt the two, having the desire to depart and be with Christ; for it is very far better: yet to abide in the flesh is more needful for your sake" (Phil. 1:21, 23-24).

The apostle Peter also wrote concerning Christ's resurrection and its significance for us. "Blessed be the God and Father of our Lord Jesus Christ, who according to his great mercy begat us again unto a living hope by the resurrection of Jesus Christ from the dead, unto an inheritance incorruptible, and undefiled, and that fadeth not away, reserved in heaven for you, who by the power of God are guarded through faith unto a salvation ready to be revealed in the last time. Wherein ye greatly rejoice . . ." (I Peter 1:3-6).

The Old Testament psalmist wrote, "Precious in the sight of Jehovah is the death of his saints" (116:15). In the final book of the Bible is a parallel statement: "Blessed are the dead who die in the Lord from henceforth: yea, saith the Spirit, that they may rest from their labors; for their works follow with them" (14:13). Also in Revelation are these hope-filled words: "He shall wipe away every tear from their eyes; and death shall be no more; neither shall there be mourning, nor crying, nor pain, any more: the first things are passed away" (21:4). On the basis of these great promises of a better life beyond death, the Christian faces death in confidence and hope rather than in doubt and despair.

Obviously, our hope of being raised from the dead lies in the resurrection of our Lord.

Helping Others Face Death

Men grieve over lost causes, lost opportunities, broken friendships, broken homes, and, of course, death. They reach, often blindly, for help. God's people should assist them in finding solace, if not immediate solutions, by means of the comfort and hope that are present in Christ. Christ alone can heal man's deepest hurts. The thoughtful, concerned Christian can greatly help those who face death, either their own or that of someone in their family circle. And, incidentally, the Christian finds that in helping others he often helps himself—for he is not immune to the world's ills.

Sometimes when death has taken someone from our family, we need to let our emotions have their way. It is far better to face the loss of a beloved parent or life companion openly and honestly than it is to contain the grief within and give no outward sign that anything of significance has happened. Open honesty is always the wisest course. By shedding tears and openly admitting grief, one often finds a release and can begin to adjust to this new situation.

Some years ago Richard Wilke conducted a funeral service for a man whose youngest son, because he was a new recruit in the army, had been unable to see his father during the brief illness before his death. For some reason the family kept up a pretense of near gaiety at the funeral, creating a superficial air of unreality that pervaded the atmosphere, and the eighteen-year-old soldier seemed dazed. Wilke later said, "I knew the boy well, and after the graveside service, when he was standing by himself, I walked up to him, my hand on his shoulder, and said: 'John, I'm sorry.' A big tear welled up in each eye, but before those two tears had time to hit the ground, a sister-in-law rushed over, grabbed him by the arm and frantically 'rescued' him with trivial chatter." How tragic, for here was a man, standing beside his father's grave, who was not even allowed to shed a tear. Some things are so deep and so significant that it is right and proper to respond emotionally. Death is certainly one of them. Sometimes we can be very helpful to a bereaved husband or wife, but only if we share their sorrow, allowing them to express their deepest feelings of heartache and loss. Then, there comes a time when we can turn their thoughts toward the rebuilding process and strengthen them for that.

It seems strange, but an almost universal misconception is that one should avoid mentioning to the bereaved their recently deceased child or parent, husband or wife, because it might make them sorrowful. Quite often, it will make them just the opposite. One person told of riding in a car with a couple and a woman who had lost her husband the year before; the two couples had been close friends, had gone to church together, and had enjoyed many of the same hobbies. The man remembered something funny that had happened to the four of them and started to tell about it. Suddenly he stopped and said, "I'm sorry." The widow replied, "Don't be sorry. For a year, nobody has even mentioned his name in my presence. I'd love to laugh as we once laughed together!" Deep satisfaction often comes from talking about those whom we have loved so deeply with sympathetic, interested friends. It helps to make the loss seem less complete.

After death has come, close family members often experience feelings of guilt for some thoughtless act, some angry word, some little neglect. These loom large, out of all proportion, and cause the bereaved deep anguish. It is a time for an intimate friend to remind the one who is suffering of his many words of kindness and acts of love for the one who has gone. These far outweigh those few words and acts that are so deeply regretted. Who does not wish he could undo some wrong things? Who is there who, if he had a chance, would not perform some undone acts of love? All of us find it hard to say, "I'm sorry," and, "I love you," often enough.

When an older person dies, we usually feel less grief because we know that they had a rich, full, and rewarding life. But what of the death not of the old, the tired, and the philosophical, but of the little child, or the bride-to-be, or the young husband and provider, or the desperately needed mother. No glib expressions of comfort will do. Sometimes a handclasp and a period of silence can be more helpful than many words. It is a time to be reminded of God's love and a time to lean upon God who cares. Scriptures like the eighth chapter of Romans come to mind: "And we know that to them that love God all things work together for good . . ." (v. 28). A little later in the same chapter he wrote, "Who shall separate us from the love of Christ? shall tribulation, or anguish, or persecution, or famine, or nakedness, or peril, or sword? . . . Nay, in all these things we are more than conquerors through him that loved us" (vv. 35, 37). Or perhaps Paul's words to the Philippians are needed: "In nothing be anxious; but in everything by prayer and supplication with thanksgiving let your requests be made known unto God. And the peace of God, which passeth all understanding, shall guard your hearts and your thoughts in Christ Jesus" (4:6, 7). A moment later Paul added, "I can do all things in him that strengtheneth me" (v. 13).

Sometimes we can do nothing except hope and pray. We

certainly ought to hope as long as we can and to pray earnestly that God will do whatever is best. When we ourselves face critical illness, or when some member of the family faces death, we need to pray, "May my life be spared," or "May the life of my loved one be spared, *if it is thy will, O God.*" We do not always know what is best. We may be asking for that which would only mean greater suffering and anguish later on. So, we wisely pray that God's will be done, whatever His will is. We then need to pray for the spiritual maturity and stamina to accept His will. There is more to prayer than merely asking for what we want.

We Know Not the Day Nor the Hour

Daniel Webster said that "one may live as a conqueror, a king, or a magistrate; but he must die a man. The bed of death brings every human being to his pure individuality, to the intense contemplation of that deepest and most solemn of all relations —the relation between the creature and his Creator." But the mature Christian does not dread death. Oh, of course, he may want to continue to live for the sake of his loved ones and his work, but the real Christian is so in tune with spiritual things and so intimate with the Lord that he neither fears nor dreads death. Each of us should strive to live in a state of readiness in case the end should come suddenly. When Christ was on the earth, He admonished His disciples, ". . . be ye also ready; for in an hour that ye think not the Son of man cometh" (Matt. 24:44). A little later He said, "Watch therefore, for ye know not the day nor the hour" (Matt. 25:13).

This means, of course, that we need to have not only the superficial things of our lives ready if the end should come suddenly, but also the deeper things. It is fine to have all of our business and personal things in good shape, but it is infinitely more important for our souls to be ready to meet God in judgment. This means that we must have become children of God, living faithful, obedient lives and serving God and our fellow men. The ideal is to believe early in life that Jesus Christ is the divine Son of God and to decide to follow Christ. This means repentance, or turning away from the world and its sin; this means the confession of Christ before men; this means obedience to the Lord's command to be baptized. Then, it means living as Christ lived—in purity and in concern for the needs of others. While it is ideal to begin early in life, it is never too late to begin. One is never too old to have a genuine desire to follow Christ, to be willing to obey Him. The only ultimate tragedy of life is to die outside of Christ. What a blessing to know that not one of us need be lost. Christ died that we might live and invites us to come to Him and to share eternal life in heaven. As the Christian faces death, he may well remember the words of the poet John Milton, "Death is the golden key that opens the palace of eternity."

11

The Resurrection

An elderly lady called on me in my study one morning recently. After introducing herself, she told me that she and her husband had often watched together our "Herald of Truth" television program before his recent death. Then came the reason for her call. She felt an overwhelming sense of loneliness and asked, "Do you think we will know each other over on the other side of death?"

Earnest Questions

So many times over the years people have asked me such questions as these: Will we know each other over there? Will we have the same bodies that we've had here on earth? If so, what about those who have lost fingers, arms, and legs? What about those organs removed by the surgeon's knife? What about the billions of people whose physical bodies have returned to the dust? So puzzling and unreal to us is the spiritual world to come that we sometimes find it difficult to put into words the questions that come to our minds.

Certainly this generation is not the first to ask questions about

111

death and the life beyond. In the Book of Job, which undoubtedly refers to one of the earliest periods mentioned in the Bible, we find these words: "Man, that is born of a woman, Is of few days, and full of trouble. He cometh forth like a flower, and is cut down: He fleeth also as a shadow and continueth not" (14: 1, 2). A moment later Job asked, "If a man die, shall he live again?" (v. 14)

This interesting incident is told in Matthew's Gospel:

> On that day there came to him Sadducees, they that say there is no resurrection: and they asked him, saying, Teacher, Moses said, If a man die, having no children, his brother shall marry his wife, and raise up seed unto his brother. [This was the law of levirate marriage.] Now there were with us seven brethren: and the first married and deceased, and having no seed left his wife unto his brother; in like manner the second also, and the third, unto the seventh. And after them all, the woman died. In the resurrection therefore whose wife shall she be of the seven? for they all had her. But Jesus answered and said unto them, Ye do err, not knowing the scriptures, nor the power of God. For in the resurrection they neither marry, nor are given in marriage, but are as angels in heaven. But as touching the resurrection of the dead, have ye not read that which was spoken unto you by God, saying, I am the God of Abraham, and the God of Isaac, and the God of Jacob? God is not the God of the dead, but of the living. And when the multitudes heard it, they were astonished at his teaching. [22:23-33]

Sadducees, who were open opponents of Christ while he was on earth and who believed that there was no resurrection and no life beyond the grave, framed this hypothetical situation in order to disprove Jesus' teaching concerning the resurrection. In answering their question Christ taught at least three things quite clearly: first, there is a resurrection after death; second, in that new life the physical relationships of husband and wife no longer exist, for "they neither marry, nor are given in marriage, but are as angels in heaven"; third, people do, however, retain their identity, since Abraham, Isaac, and Jacob continue to exist. At an earlier time Jesus said, "And I say unto you, that many shall come from the east and the west, and shall sit down with

Abraham, and Isaac, and Jacob, in the kingdom of heaven . . ."
(Matt. 8:11). If they retain their identity, so will we.

Some years after the church was established, the apostle Paul
went to Athens, the intellectual capital of the ancient world, and
preached Christ and the resurrection of the dead. As the histor-
ian Luke told the story, ". . . certain also of the Epicurean and
Stoic philosophers encountered him. And some said, What would
this babbler say? others, He seemeth to be a setter forth of
strange gods: because he preached Jesus and the resurrection.
And they took hold of him, and brought him unto the Areo-
pagus, saying, May we know what this new teaching is, which
is spoken by thee?" Then Paul preached his famous sermon on
Mars Hill, in which he revealed the true and living God. Toward
the end of his sermon he said: "The times of ignorance therefore God overlooked; but now he commandeth men that they
should all everywhere repent: inasmuch as he hath appointed a
day in which he will judge the world in righteousness by the
man whom he hath ordained; whereof he hath given assurance
unto all men, in that he hath raised him from the dead. Now
when they heard of the resurrection of the dead, some mocked;
but others said, We will hear thee concerning this yet again"
(Acts 17:18, 19, 30-32). Even the very learned Athenians
were eager to learn more about this interesting subject of life
after death.

Apart from our Lord Jesus Christ there can be no ultimate
victory. With Christ all things are possible, including forgiveness of sins, resurrection from the dead, and eternal salvation in
heaven. This is the perfect peace to which believers are called.

Christ's Resurrection

No Christian tenet is more fundamental than Christ's resurrection from the dead. The apostles and other preachers of the
early church declared it everywhere. For example, Paul wrote to
the Corinthians: "Now I make known unto you, brethren, the
gospel which I preached unto you, which also ye received,
wherein also ye stand, by which also ye are saved, if ye hold fast
the word which I preached unto you, except ye believed in vain.
For I delivered unto you first of all that which also I received:

that Christ died for our sins according to the scriptures; and that he was buried; and that he hath been raised on the third day according to the scriptures . . ." (I Cor. 15:1-4). A moment later he added, "Now if Christ is preached that he hath been raised from the dead, how say some among you that there is no resurrection of the dead? But if there is no resurrection of the dead, neither hath Christ been raised: and if Christ hath not been raised, then is our preaching vain, your faith also is vain . . . If we have only hoped in Christ in this life, we are of all men most pitiable. But now hath Christ been raised from the dead, the firstfruits of them that are asleep" (15:12-14, 19, 20).

The early Christians held the firm conviction that Christ was raised from the dead, because many of those who saw Him die saw Him alive again. Christ appeared on a dozen or more occasions to various individuals and groups. They recognized Him as the precrucifixion Lord whom they had known so intimately. Yet, certain characteristics of His resurrected body were different from His physical body prior to His death and resurrection. For example, He appeared to the apostles in an upper room the doors of which were locked. Yet, His body retained the nail-holes in His hands and the spear-wound in His side. While it was the same body that had died and been buried, it was also different in certain important respects.

The conviction that Jesus was raised from the dead was further established in the minds of the early Christians by the empty tomb. The body which had been killed by the Roman soldiers on the cross and laid in the tomb of Joseph of Arimathea could not be found there three days later. The tomb was empty. Although the enemies of Christ fabricated stories about His disciples stealing His body, their claims were not convincing. How could the disciples have stolen the body from a tomb carefully sealed with a stone and guarded by soldiers? Even more significant is the fact that the disciples returned to Jerusalem after the crucifixion disheartened, ready to give up, because they thought their Lord's cause had died with His death on the cross. Yet, three days later and for the remainder of their lives, they were willing to go everywhere preaching the story of Christ's resurrection, even at the cost of their lives. Only a resurrected Lord could have so changed their attitudes. Men do not die for a hoax.

The early Christians did not preach the resurrection of Christ merely as a fact of history. The early Christians preached the resurrection as gospel to sinful men, who were separated from God. The glorious fact that Christ had risen triumphantly from the grave brought encouragement and hope to fallen men that they might be empowered to live again. The Christian's hope derives its meaning from Christ's triumphant resurrection. If the resurrection did not occur, the gospel of Christ loses its reality and force. Christ is the "firstfruits," which implies other fruit will follow. Christ's resurrection opens the door of hope for all of us.

More than a hundred years ago Sarah Adams wrote the lovely poem in which the line occurs,

> E'en though it be a cross that raiseth me;
> Still all my song shall be, nearer, my God, to thee.

Our Resurrection

The idea of a general resurrection for all men is taught throughout the Scriptures, though more clearly in the New Testament than in the Old. But even in the Old Testament we read: "And many of them that sleep in the dust of the earth shall awake, some to everlasting life, and some to shame and everlasting contempt" (Dan. 12:2); and, in the words of Solomon, "The dust returneth to the earth as it was, and the spirit returneth unto God who gave it" (Eccles. 12:7)

Christ declared the resurrection of all men plainly. On one occasion he said, "Marvel not at this: for the hour cometh, in which all that are in the tombs shall hear his voice, and shall come forth; they that have done good, unto the resurrection of life; and they that have done evil, unto the resurrection of judgment" (John 5:28-29). A little later he added, "This is the will of my Father, that everyone that beholdeth the Son, and believeth on him, should have eternal life; and I will raise him up at the last day" (6:40). To Martha, the sister of Lazarus, Jesus said, "Thy brother shall rise again. Martha saith unto him, I know that he shall rise again in the resurrection at the last day. Jesus said unto her, I am the resurrection, and the life: he that believeth on me, though he die, yet shall he live; and whosoever liveth and believeth on me shall never die. Believest thou this?" (John 11:23-26).

No passage in all of the New Testament says as much about the resurrection of the body as the fifteenth chapter of I Corinthians, in which Paul wrote:

> But some one will say, How are the dead raised? and with what manner of body do they come? Thou foolish one, that which thou thyself sowest is not quickened except it die: and that which thou sowest, thou sowest not the body that shall be, but a bare grain, it may chance of wheat, or of some other kind; but God giveth it a body even as it pleased him, and to each seed a body of its own. All flesh is not the same flesh: but there is one flesh of men, and another flesh of beasts, and another flesh of birds, and another of fishes. There are also celestial bodies, and bodies terrestrial: but the glory of the celestial is one, and the glory of the terrestrial is another. There is one glory of the sun, and another glory of the moon, and another glory of the stars; for one star differeth from another star in glory. So also is the resurrection of the dead. It is sown in corruption; it is raised in incorruption: it is sown in dishonor; it is raised in glory: it is sown in weakness; it is raised in power: it is sown a natural body; it is raised a spiritual body. If there is a natural body, there is also a spiritual body. [vv. 35-44]

Paul continued,

> Now this I say, brethren, that flesh and blood cannot inherit the kingdom of God; neither doth corruption inherit incorruption. Behold, I tell you a mystery: We all shall not sleep, but we shall all be changed, in a moment, in the twinkling of an eye, at the last trump: for the trumpet shall sound, and the dead shall be raised incorruptible, and we shall be changed. For this corruptible must put on incorruption, and this mortal must put on immortality . . . then shall come to pass the saying that is written, Death is swallowed up in victory. [vv. 50-54]

The idea of the resurrection of the physical body fascinated Paul's contemporaries as much as it does us. To some Palestinian believers resurrection meant merely that the same body that was buried would be restored. One early writer stated confidently, "The earth will . . . assuredly restore the dead . . . making no change in their form, but as it has received, so will it restore them." Obviously, in view of I Corinthians 15, the apostle Paul did not teach this. He taught that the physical body dies and is buried, and some kind of spiritual body is raised. Paul used an analogy: we plant a seed; we get back an entirely different form. Paul also spoke of the many different forms that God has given to the various types of life—human beings, animals, birds, fish. He also referred to the different kinds of celestial bodies, which also demonstrate great variety. His point is simply that God expertly gives the kind of body that is needed. Hence, we can trust Him to provide the kind of spiritual body needed for a spiritual world.

Rather than becoming disturbed over the kind of body we will have in the resurrection, Paul advises us to trust God, who has so expertly fashioned the various forms that we can know and observe in this life, to give us the kind of body we will need in the life to come. Whatever it is like, it will not be the same expendable earthly body which we know here, but rather a spiritual body partaking of the nature of God's own heavenly glory. We get some inkling of God's ability to transform life when we study the garden caterpillar which, through the process of metamorphosis, is transformed into the beautiful butterfly. If God can work this change, then surely He can take care of our needs in the resurrection.

In his second Corinthian letter Paul put the matter in these words: "For we know that if the earthly house of our tabernacle be dissolved, we have a building from God, a house not made with hands, eternal, in the heavens" (5:1). In his Philippian letter he referred to God fashioning "anew the body of our humiliation, that it may be conformed to the body of his glory, according to the working whereby he is able even to subject all things unto himself" (3:21). In his first Thessalonian letter Paul encouraged the Christians with these words:

> But we would not have you ignorant, brethren, concerning them that fall asleep; that ye sorrow not, even as the rest, who have no hope. For if we believe that Jesus died and rose again, even

so them also that are fallen asleep in Jesus will God bring with him. For this we say unto you by the word of the Lord, that we that are alive, that are left unto the coming of the Lord, shall in no wise precede them that are fallen asleep. For the Lord himself shall descend from heaven, with a shout, with the voice of the archangel, and with the trump of God: and the dead in Christ shall rise first; then we that are alive, that are left, shall together with them be caught up in the clouds, to meet the Lord in the air: and so shall we ever be with the Lord. [4:13-17]

An Epitaph and a Poem

Before his death Benjamin Franklin prepared this epitaph to be used on his grave:

The Body

of

Benjamin Franklin, Printer,

(Like the cover of an old book,

Its contents torn out,

And stripped of its lettering and gilding,)

Lies here food for worms.

Yet the work itself shall not be lost,

For it will (as he believes) appear once

more

In a new

And more beautiful Edition

Corrected and Amended

by

The Author

"Death," wrote Harry Emerson Fosdick, "is a great adventure . . . The man of faith may face it as Columbus faced his first voyage from the shores of Spain. What lies across the sea, he cannot tell; his special expectations all may be mistaken; but his insight into the clear meanings of the present facts may persuade him beyond doubt that the sea has another shore. Such confident faith, so founded upon reasonable grounds, shall be turned to sight when, for all the disbelief of the unbelieving, the hope of the seers is rewarded by the vision of a new continent."

One of my early teachers, nearly forty years ago, was a remarkable man named Charles R. Brewer. He was a noted educator, preacher, and author. He lived well into his eightieth year. One who knew him well remarked at his funeral, "He was the only man I ever knew who reached his very zenith in his eightieth year." I think it can be safely said that he was not concerned about the state in which he would be raised. He was satisfied to leave this matter in the hands of his Creator. He believed he would be raised from the dead, as had the apostle Paul before him who said, "For if we have become united with him in the likeness of his death, we shall be also in the likeness of his resurrection" (Rom. 6:5). Some few months before his death, this grand old man whose ministry had covered more than sixty years found a quiet time and wrote a remarkable poem entitled "A Post-Dated Prayer."

Dear Father-God: The time may come when I will be too busy dying
To turn sane thoughts to thee, and number all good things you've done for me;
Or if I call thy name, it may be only inarticulate cries of pain
From stammering lips and dulling brain. Senses wracked in fear having little room
For thoughts of blessings that have come: The heart is so intent on beating
And mortal life holds on so stubbornly that it would forfeit all treasures past
Of future hopes just to keep on going for a few more fleeting days.
Not so, Lord, would I be. And so, I ask thee now to close thine ears
To any frantic calls that I may make for help or extension of my time:
But rather Lord, please file this plea away, and in infinite mercy on that last day
Accept it as my final prayer to thee.
And so, before that hour arrives, while still my mind is clear,
My body free from pain, let me say, Thank you, thank you, thank you Lord,

Again and yet again! For all unspeakable joys attendant
On my journey-road of life: For all the blessings of my years
I give thee thanks and praise: For bitter-sweet of love and tears,
Long memories of childhood days, For dreams of youth, and
    testing hours,
When 'twas thy hand that guided me, and I was kept within
    thy power
From pitfalls that I did not see.
For happy years of wedded life, for gentle, sweet and faithful
    wife,
For stalwart sons, strong in the faith, a daughter-dear brought
    by a breath
From heaven—a jewel rare in answer to a long, long prayer.
Bless them Lord, and help them to be through all their life-
    days true to thee,
Give them wisdom, grace and power sufficient for each trying
    hour,
Help them with pride to wear the name, not mine, but thine,
Born not of my blood, but of that blood that made them
    children of the living God.
For the lovely world, your guest-house, in which you've let
    me stay so long
I thank thee; for every night and day,
For morning dawn and sunset glory that reach within the heart
    and stir feelings
Beyond the realm of speech, and all the festive board of
    nature-love
Where day by day I've shared thy manna from above.
For fellowship of friends whose faith in me has helped my own
    faith stronger be.
For all these blessings, Lord, and Oh, so many more Let me
    say, Thank you, thank you, even now, and o'er and o'er.
Blot out the spots, O Lord, spots on the sun, made dimmer by
    the wrongs I've done.
Forgive them and in mercy move all shades of night, And in
    this evening hour
Oh Lord, let there be light, that I, now looking back, may
    sure know

The love that cleanses white as snow.

So as you see me now in this post-dated hour, my body torn
by demon-life

So loathe to let me go, please, God, as once you healed the
wretched lad so long ago

Even so bid now my striving cease, and let my ransomed soul
come home in peace.

And here I would like to turn again to the Scripture: ". . . according to the power of God; who saved us, and called us with a holy calling, not according to our works, but according to his own purpose and grace, which was given us in Christ Jesus before times eternal, but hath now been manifested by the appearing of our Saviour Christ Jesus, who abolished death, and brought life and immortality to light through the gospel" (II Tim. 1:8-10).

I do not fear death, nor do I have any serious questions about the life to come in that more wonderful world which Christ is preparing for His disciples. My only concern is that each of us may so know the Lord and so follow Him that we will be ready when He returns to call His followers to that better world. Rather than being burdensome, obedience to Christ's commands is a joy because in such obedience we are preparing to spend eternity in heaven with God our Creator.

12

The Deeper Purpose
of Life

Who am I? Why am I here? Whence did I come? Where am I going? These are the questions a man must answer if he would learn the deeper purpose of life. Man, because God breathed into his nostrils the breath of life, is a living soul (Gen. 2:7). He is not a "mere collocation of atoms" as the late Bertrand Russell concluded. Because man is a responsible being, he must find his Maker and seek the things that are above.

Dr. Vannevar Bush, one of the nation's top scientists, has written a very challenging book entitled *Science Is Not Enough*. In this scientific twentieth century, when some men are prone to think that science can answer every question, it is helpful to find a topflight scientist with a broader and more comprehensive view of existence. Dr. Bush writes:

A philosophy of [eighteenth- and nineteenth-century] materialism [led man to believe he] would be able to understand all of nature . . . Everything would be controlled by a neat set of equations. Merely by observing the present state of things, one could predict all the future. All the history of the universe, all of man's part in it, was, so it seemed, controlled by causal, mechanistic

122

laws. Man was merely an automaton. His fancied choice of acts was an illusion; he merely carried out what was inevitable in the light of his nature and nurture. Pride of intellect never went further . . .

To this materialistic explanation of life, Dr. Bush reacted this way:

Science has come a long way in delineating the probable nature of the universe that surrounds us, of the physical world in which we live, of our own structure, our physical and chemical nature. It even enters into the mechanism by which the brain operates. Then it comes to the question of consciousness and free will— and there it stops. No longer can science prove, or even bear evidence . . . He who follows science blindly, and who follows it alone, comes to a barrier beyond which he cannot see . . . and on the essential and central core of faith, science will of necessity be silent . . . But its silence will be the silence of humility, not the silence of disdain . . . Young men who will formulate the deep thought of the next generation, should lean on science, for it can teach much and it can inspire. But they should not lean where it does not apply.

A Spiritual Realm, Too

It is deeply gratifying to hear a leading scientist declare openly that, as great as have been the achievements of science in the material realm, science has nothing to say in the spiritual or religious realm. This is no reflection upon science. It is an acknowledgement that one cannot ask: How much does love weigh? How many miles long is honesty? What color is peace? Obviously, one cannot measure the concepts of love, honesty, and peace in terms of physical weight, length, or color. Science has many answers, but only in the material universe, not in the ethical, moral, and spiritual realm.

Blaise Pascal, whom many of us may remember as both the father of the computing machine and the founder of the theory of probability, or Pascal's Law, was another leading scientist who recognized the importance of the spiritual. He wrote, "Without Jesus Christ the world could not continue in being. It would necessarily work its own destruction, or else it would become a kind of hell." His statement is a prophecy that seems to come closer and closer to fulfillment as man discovers more about the universe around him and, at the same time, is less concerned about the guidance of his Lord.

As a case in point, listen to Bertrand Russell's extremely despondent description of life:

> That man is the product of causes which had no prevision of the end they were achieving; that his origin, his growth, his hopes and fears, his loves and his beliefs, are but the outcome of accidental collocations of atoms; that no fire, no heroism, no intensity of thought and feeling, can preserve an individual life beyond the grave; that all the labors of the ages, all the devotion, all the inspiration, all the noonday brightness of the human genius, are destined to extinction in the vast death of the solar system and that the whole temple of man's achievement must inevitably be buried beneath the debris of a universe in ruins—all of these things, if not quite beyond dispute, are yet so nearly certain, that no philosophy which rejects them can hope to stand.

With all his brilliance, Bertrand Russell failed to comprehend the deeper purpose of life, leaving him with a futile, depressing view of life.

On the one hand is scientist Bush's view that behind the physical elements of existence is a deeper meaning, and on the other is philosopher Russell's view that the physical is all there is. Each of us must decide whether this deeper meaning exists.

I am convinced that we Christians ought to be quite ready to examine our faith. Actually, an unexamined faith is not worth having. We must be deeply concerned to know that it is true, not merely that it is pleasant or nice. To borrow the words of Elton Trueblood: "We must reject utterly the sometimes popular notion that religion thrives on ignorance, capitalizing on those areas which are unknown. If this were accepted, the area of religious reality would be diminished every time a new scientific discovery is made. This would be both undignified and intolerable. Since valid faith is built not on what is not, but on that which is, the honest religious thinker welcomes knowledge of every kind. Ignorance is not revealing, but knowledge is."

Then, there is the statement of William Lyon Phelps of Yale:

"My religious faith remains in possession of the field only after prolonged civil war with my naturally skeptical mind." I am convinced that the Christian view of life will withstand the most careful scrutiny. Life becomes meaningful only when one understands the deeper purpose behind it, and one understands that deeper purpose only when he knows Christ.

The Unseen Hand of God

Horace Bushnell, in his famous sermon, "Every Man's Life a Plan of God," championed the cause that behind the outward, visible acts and events of life is the unseen but very real hand of God. This is also the view of the Spirit-guided apostle Paul: ". . . for there is no power but of God; and the powers that be are ordained of God" (Rom. 13:1). Bushnell said in his sermon that

> Christ himself testifies to the girding of the Almighty, when He says, "To this end was I born, and for this cause came I into the world" (John 18:37). Abraham was girded for a particular work and mission, in what is otherwise denominated his call. Joseph, in Egypt, distinguishes the girding of God's hand, when he comforts his guilty brothers in the assurance, "So, it was not you that sent me hither, but God" (Genesis 45:8). Moses and Samuel were even called by name, and sent to their great life work in the same manner. And what is Paul endeavoring, in all the stress and pressure of his mighty apostleship, but to perform the work for which God's Spirit girded him at his call, and to apprehend that for which he was apprehended of Christ Jesus?

Let us notice a few statements in the Scriptures themselves which indicate the existence of an overruling divine purpose behind events. Joseph said to his brothers, whose lives were in his hands: ". . . Fear not: for am I in the place of God? And as for you, ye meant evil against me; but God meant it for good, to bring to pass, as it is this day, to save much people alive" (Gen. 50:19, 20).

In I Samuel is this description of God's activity in the affairs of men: "Jehovah killeth, and maketh alive: He bringeth down to Sheol, and bringeth up. Jehovah maketh poor and maketh rich: He bringeth low, he also lifteth up. He raiseth up the poor out of the dust, He lifteth up the needy from the dunghill, To make them sit with princes, And inherit the throne of glory: For the pillars of the earth are Jehovah's, And he hath set the world upon them" (2:6-8). David said in one of his psalms: "Let all the earth fear Jehovah: Let all the inhabitants of the world stand in awe of him. For he spake, and it was done; He commanded, and it stood fast. Jehovah bringeth the counsel of the nations to nought; He maketh the thoughts of the peoples to be of no effect . . . Blessed is the nation whose God is Jehovah . . . Jehovah looketh from heaven; He beholdeth all the sons of men" (33:8-10, 12, 13). Perhaps more often quoted is this statement from Psalm 127: "Except Jehovah build the house, They labor in vain that build it; Except Jehovah keep the city, The watchman waketh but in vain" (v. 1). The apostle Paul gave evidence of his firm faith that God's purpose had molded the events of his life: "Now I would have you know, brethren, that the things which happened unto me have fallen out rather unto the progress of the gospel; so that my bonds became manifest in Christ throughout the whole praetorian guard, and to all the rest" (Phil. 1:12, 13). Paul also gave us the most familiar of all statements of the providence of God: ". . . we know that to them that love God all things work together for good, even to them that are called according to his purpose" (Rom. 8:28). All of these passages say with great clarity that life is more than accidental, unplanned, unguided events; God is actively working in history.

The believer does not minimize trials and difficulties, with which life is filled. He relies, rather, on the strength offered by his Lord.

Superiority of the Inner Realm

One of the most thoughtful teachers under whom it was my privilege to study was Dr. E. H. Ijams. I still remember the almost hypnotic effect upon us students in our high school and early college years as he taught some of the great principles of Christian living. Many years later, when he was eighty years of age, he wrote a very meaningful book, *Power to Survive and*

Surpass. In it he pointed out a very significant difference between the Hebrews and the Greeks:

> As respects Hebrew thinking, it should be noted that it does not stress the importance of environment as do Greek and scientific thought. Primarily the Hebrews were concerned, not with physical environment, but with what was behind it—the creative presence, sovereignty, and glory of God. To the Hebrews, "the ultimate," the "First Cause," was not as with the Greeks, an abstract something, but the living God. To them, man's highest goal was not to master his physical and human environment but to live justly and nobly among men, and to walk humbly with God (Micah 6:8). Their great plea was, "Fear God and keep his commandments" (Ecclesiastes 12:13). For those so doing, they believed God would provide a beneficent environment. Blessedness, according to the Hebrews, is achieved through moral righteousness and through the faithful observance of all divine statutes and ordinances. The Greeks, on the other hand, had no divinely revealed laws in the Hebrew sense. The big thing with them was the greatness and freedom of mind. In practice, their thoughts centered on adjustment to environment, not on what is beyond it. They gloried in the values of intellect, order, and aesthetics. In what we today call the arts and sciences, the Greeks of the fourth and third centuries before Christ reached an all-time high. But it is worth repeating that they never quite grasped the secret of man's highest personal and social possibilities.

In contrast to the Greek view, wrote Dr. Ijams, was Christ's primary emphasis:

> Jesus was not content only to *give* great gifts. Above all else, he strove to cause man to *become* something greater—vastly greater—than what he can be by nature . . . Inward life, said Jesus, is the supreme gift or value. And he came that people might have, not culture or science only, but that they might have life, and have it abundantly (John 10:10).

The apostle Paul, following the lead of his Lord, emphasized the "inward man" over the "outer man." In his second Corinthian letter, he wrote: "Wherefore we faint not; but though our outward man is decaying, yet our inward man is renewed day by day. For our light affliction, which is for the moment, worketh for us more and more exceedingly an eternal weight of glory; while we look not at the things which are seen, but at the things which are not seen; for the things which are seen are temporal; but the things which are not seen are eternal. For we know that if the earthly house of our tabernacle be dissolved, we have a building from God, a house not made with hands, eternal, in the heavens" (4:16 -5:1). In one of his famous prayers he prayed that the Ephesians "may be strengthened with power through his Spirit in the inward man . . ." (3:16). In this particular prayer he said nothing at all about the outer man. Just as the inner, spiritual man is more important than the outer, physical man, so the deeper purpose behind the universe is more important than the more obvious events of physical nature. Life has a deeper purpose.

The Ultimate Questions

To the question with which we began, "What is man?" there are essentially two answers: (1) man is, as he delights to say, a kind of mechanism controlled by digestive and economic needs, an animal closely related to the ape or monkey; (2) man is, as the Bible says, created by God "but little lower than God," and is crowned "with glory and honor." Man was created "to have dominion over the works of thy hands; Thou hast put all things under his feet" (Ps. 8:4-6).

To the second question, "Why is man here?" many answer that man came into being out of the nothingness of mindless matter and reached his present state through incredibly long years of groping and developing—from the lesser to the greater. This completely disregards the undisputed fact of entropy, not to mention the Bible record, according to which man was placed here by God, the Creator, and given the unfathomable power of endlessness (Heb. 7:16). But that power was conditional; man had to love God, glorify God, believe God, and serve God.

To the question, "Where is man going?" the skeptic has no answer, and he freely admits it. The Scriptures give a very clear answer. "And the dust returneth to the earth as it was, and the spirit returneth unto God who gave it" (Eccles. 12:7). "And I saw the dead, the great and the small, standing before the throne; and books were opened; and another book was opened, which is the book of life: and the dead were judged out of the things which were written in the books, according to their works . . . And death and Hades were cast into the lake of fire. This is the second death, even the lake of fire. And if any was not found written in the book of life, he was cast into the lake of fire" (Rev. 20:12, 14-15). "These shall go away into eternal punishment: but the righteous into eternal life" (Matt. 25:46). The last statement was made by the Lord himself.

Apart from God, man must cross a dark abyss on a slippery log. There is a safe highway, but it is narrow. The living God pleads through His prophet: "Seek ye Jehovah while he may be found; call ye upon him while he is near: let the wicked forsake his way, and the unrighteous man his thoughts; and let him return unto Jehovah, and he will have mercy upon him; and to our God, for he will abundantly pardon" (Isa. 55:6, 7). Jesus, the Incarnate One, pleads, "Come unto me, all ye that labor and are heavy laden, and I will give you rest. Take my yoke upon you, and learn of me; for I am meek and lowly in heart; and ye shall find rest unto your souls" (Matt. 11:28, 29).

In the Bible God reveals to us why we are here, where we originated, and where we are going. He reveals that we have one of two destinations and that we must choose. The choice of eternal life with our Lord involves implicit faith, a faith that involves a willingness to repent of our sins; to confess the name of Jesus as Lord and Christ, the Son of the living God; to be baptized in the name of the Father, Son, and Holy Spirit for the remission of sins; and to serve the Lord, fully committed to His cause, till death.

13

Is Happiness

Just a Word?

The world is full of sorrow and suffering. Beautiful dreams fade in the light of harsh reality. We live in a demanding world where pain and disappointment assault the mind as well as the body. Discouragement lurks behind every worthwhile endeavor. Eventually we have to ask ourselves, "Is happiness just a word?" I am confident it is much more than a word.

According to the best estimates available, the earth is now inhabited by some three and one-half billion people. Different though we may be, we have many things in common: all of us have been born and all of us will die, unless the end of time should come first; we all eat and sleep and work; we love our families and friends; we experience joy and sorrow. We are alike in many other ways, too. However, nothing is more common or more universal than the desire to be happy. We all seek happiness.

To many millions of people, however, happiness is only a word. They've heard of it, but they have never achieved it, and its achievement appears impossible. Many seek it and few find it. It is elusive. We are led to ask, "Is happiness only a word—

130

an impossible dream?" I think not, and I believe that every man can achieve it who really wants it.

What Is Happiness?

But perhaps we ought to ask, "What is happiness?" Dr. Maxwell Maltz, in his book *Five Minutes to Happiness,* gives this answer: "Happiness is a state of mind or habit where we have pleasant thoughts the greater part of the time. It is a built-in mechanism within us." After I first read this paragraph, I reflected that many people seem to have everything to make them happy, but are not happy; and that others have few of the ingredients of happiness, but somehow are happy. Dr. Maltz continues: "To understand this better it might be well to realize that we also have a built-in worry mechanism. These are not two separate entities like two ears on the face, but they are interlocking processes that work daily in our lives, expressing our emotions, and when we begin to understand who we are, we alone can decide which mechanism we want to use for our purposes, because we can control them. We can make a habit of worrying or of being happy."

An anonymous writer has added: "Happiness and Trouble stand at everyone's gate. Yours is the choice which you will invite in." Although this view of happiness is far from comprehensive, I am convinced that everyone can be happy if he makes up his mind to be happy. More especially, I am convinced that a person who knows the teachings of Christ understands how to have a happy and meaningful life.

The greatest love story ever told is just one short sentence long, but it insures man's hope and happiness: "For God so loved the world, that he gave his only begotten Son, that whosoever believeth on him should not perish, but have eternal life" (John 3:16). The love of God reaches out to all mankind and promises far-reaching and unending joy.

Six Observations

I should like to make six observations concerning happiness.

These observations have not arisen suddenly, or even recently, but have developed gradually through the years.

Happiness is never found in wealth, power, knowledge, or physical, sensual enjoyment. Not that there is no enjoyment in the things that money can buy; not that great power and influence may not be heart-warming and gratifying; not that the accumulation of great knowledge is devoid of any satisfaction and happiness; not that there are no joys in the realm of the physical senses; but that, if one makes one or another of these areas his chief end in life, he will be disappointed ultimately. Each has a legitimate place, but none belongs in the center of our lives.

No man sought happiness with more ingenuity and persistence than Solomon. He tried all of these avenues and found them wanting. In his book Ecclesiastes we read:

> I made me great works; I builded me houses; I planted me vineyards; I made me gardens and parks, and I planted trees in them of all kinds of fruit; I made me pools of water, to water therefrom the forests where trees were reared; I bought men-servants and maid-servants, and had servants born in my house; also I had great possessions of herds and flocks, above all that were before me in Jerusalem; I gathered me also silver and gold, and the treasure of kings and of the provinces; I gat me men-singers and women-singers, and the delights of the sons of men, musical instruments, and that of all sorts. So I was great, and increased more than all that were before me in Jerusalem ... And whatsoever mine eyes desired I kept not from them; I withheld not my heart from any joy ... Then I looked on all the works that my hands had wrought, and on the labor that I had labored to do; and, behold, all was vanity and a striving after wind, and there was no profit under the sun. [2:4-11]

Happiness often is found in simple things: a boy and his dog; the pure love of a young man and woman; a sunrise or sunset; a glass of cool, clear water; the singing of birds; a baby's smile. The most popular film shown at the New York World's Fair, which ran in 1964-65, was entitled *To Be Alive.* Of the hundreds of films produced for this fair, this one had the longest waiting lines. It was the most talked-about film at the fair, but it had no plot. It was simply a series of unrelated scenes in the lives of average people. It was simple, yet profound. It showed a little Japanese boy rushing breathlessly into a field of golden wheat, the stalks of which were almost as tall as he; a young African boy rolling a hoop down a jungle trail, looking with wide eyes at the birds and animals; a grandfather, his face lined with age, and a grandson, young and eager, fishing from a boat in a quiet pond. These and other scenes, emphasizing the beauties and joys of everyday living, impressed all viewers profoundly.

Happiness is found in worthwhile work done well. A story has survived several centuries because it still bears a significant message. Sir Christopher Wren, one of his day's most advanced architects and builders, designed and supervised construction of St. Paul's Cathedral in London during the first decade of the eighteenth century. Sir Christopher approached the building site and asked a workman, "What are you doing, my man?" The man answered, "I am laying stones." Wren walked to another part of the huge construction project and asked a second man, "What are you doing, my man?" This time the answer was, "I'm earning a living for my wife and my children." Still not satisfied, Sir Christopher asked a third man at still a different location, "What are you doing?" This man responded, "I'm building a cathedral." He, like the others, was laying stones and earning a living, but he was also doing something more. He recognized the ultimate goal of his work. He put himself into his work. He did it well.

Happiness and satisfaction are often found more in the pursuit of an objective than in its attainment. Many times we enjoy ourselves more while thinking about and working for some goal than we do once we have achieved the goal. There is joy in working for something that is worthwhile.

Happiness is found in being more concerned about others than about one's self. All of us know from our own experience and from observing others that, as upside-down and backwards as this seems, nevertheless it is true. When we forget ourselves and work for the good of others, we find greater happiness than when we seek our own satisfaction. This is what Jesus meant when he said, ". . . whosoever would become great among you shall be your minister; and whosoever would be first among you shall be your servant: even as the Son of man came not to be ministered unto, but to minister, and to give his life a ransom for many" (Matt. 20:26-28).

During my college years a graduation speaker told of an immensely rewarding experience. A lady in the church of which he was minister baked a chocolate cake and brought it to the church office, saying that she wanted him and his family to have it. He expressed his appreciation and then, since it was mid-morning and not yet time to go home for lunch, set the cake on a table beside a window which opened on a vacant lot where neighborhood children often played. During the morning he happened to notice that several boys from the not-too-well-to-do neighborhood had stopped their game and were looking longingly at the cake. On an impulse, the minister invited the boys in and shared the cake with them. It was soon gone, but the wonderful memories of a happy group of neighborhood children never left him; he told our graduating class months later that he was still enjoying the cake. A generation later, I am still enjoying a cake which I never saw or tasted. And now that I have told this generous-hearted story, people all across this land will long enjoy a cake which they never saw or tasted. How different the destiny of this cake if the preacher had kept it for himself and his family.

Ultimate happiness is found only on the spiritual level. While the physical realm has its joy and satisfaction, the highest level of happiness comes only from the spiritual realm. The reason is very simple: each of us is more a spirit being than a physical body. We were made in God's image in that each of us is a living soul, destined to exist eternally. This being true, only when we are rightly related to God can we be really, constantly happy. All of us know that, when relationships with other people go wrong, we often become unhappy. When there is tension in a family, between husband and wife or between parents and children, we feel deep pains that can cause ulcers and other physical disorders. Similarly, when something is wrong with our relationship to our Creator, we are unhappy; and when our relationship to God is what it should be, we are happy.

This is what Augustine meant when he said, "Our souls are

never at rest until they find rest in Thee." After Solomon explored many realms for happiness, he concluded that to "fear God, and keep his commandments" is "the whole duty of man" (Eccles. 12:13). Actually, the translators added the word *duty* to smooth out the sentence; it is not present in the Hebrew text. Literally, Solomon said, "This is the end of the matter; all hath been heard: Fear God, and keep his commandments; for this is the whole of man."

The man who is whole looks to God as the Father of mercies. Such a man can say, "My love to Thee grows more and more."

Christian Happiness

Whereas there is much sorrow and sadness in the world, the Bible says much about joy and happiness. For example, after Jesus had taught His disciples a number of principles of righteous living, he said, "These things have I spoken unto you, that my joy may be in you, and that your joy may be made full" (John 15:11). Christ guides and instructs us so that we may be full of joy. After Pentecost, Christians, "day by day, continuing stedfastly with one accord in the temple, and breaking bread at home . . . took their food with gladness and singleness of heart" (Acts 2:46). The early Christians were happy people.

After the Ethiopian nobleman had been taught of Christ and had obeyed his Lord in baptism, "He went on his way rejoicing" (Acts 8:39). On the apostle Paul's first missionary journey, he and his disciples were driven out of the little Asian town of Lystra, but the Scripture says they "were filled with joy and with the Holy Spirit" (Acts 13:52). What unusual circumstances in which to feel joy! But these were suffering for Christ's sake. Still later, after the Philippian jailor had been converted, "he brought them [Paul and Silas, the instruments of his conversion] up into his house, and set food before them, and rejoiced greatly, with all his house, having believed in God" (Acts 16:34).

The writer of Hebrews said that we should look "unto Jesus the author and perfecter of our faith, who for the joy that was set before him endured the cross, despising shame, and hath sat down at the right hand of the throne of God" (Heb. 12:1,

2). Even in His great suffering there was joy because He was providing salvation for all men.

A great many people jest about salvation and attempt to ride roughshod over those who have accepted Christ. However, all who ridicule salvation are living without hope, and the man without hope cannot be happy. Therefore, he must find an escape from his unhappy situation. There is only one way out— the way of Christ. He calls you to faith because the alternative is condemnation (John 8:24). He calls you to repentance because the alternative is death (Luke 13:3). He calls you to confess Him before the Father in heaven (Matt. 10:32). He calls you to be baptized for the remission of your sins because the alternative is to be lost (Mark 16:16). He calls you by His gospel to "the glory of our Lord Jesus Christ" (II Thess. 2:14) because the alternative is "eternal destruction from the face of the Lord and from the glory of his might" (II Thess. 1:9). Why be a loser, an eternal loser? Why be without hope? Why be unhappy—when our Savior offers happiness to all?

To the Philippian Christians Paul wrote, "Rejoice in the Lord always" (4:4). The apostle Peter says to Christians: "Wherein ye greatly rejoice . . . at the revelation of Jesus Christ: whom not having seen ye love; on whom, though now ye see him not, yet believing, ye rejoice greatly with joy unspeakable and full of glory: receiving the end of your faith, even the salvation of your souls" (I Peter 1:6, 8, 9). This is ultimate happiness.

Finally, I would repeat the words of Jesus Himself. During His final days of teaching He spoke to His disciples about the judgment of the wicked and the salvation of the righteous, who would hear these words: "Well done, good and faithful servant: thou hast been faithful over a few things, I will set thee over many things: enter thou into the joy of thy lord" (Matt. 25:21).

Happiness is not just a word. It is a state of mind, a way of life. Happiness of the deepest sort is possible only for the Christian. G. K. Chesterton summed it all up: "Joy is the gigantic secret of the Christian."